Blended Learning Quality – Concepts Optimized for Adult Education

ISBN-10	3-901679-10-3 (PDF)
ISBN-13	978-3-901679-10-0 (PDF)
ISBN-10	3-901679-11-1 (Paperback Amazon Print-on-Demand)
ISBN-13	978-3-901679-11-7 (Paperback Amazon Print-on-Demand)
Published by	Mag. Peter Mazohl (EBI/EIE Austria)
	H.O. Staglgasse 13, A-2700 Wiener Neustadt

Project Number 539717-LLP-1-2013-1-IT-GRUNDTVIG-GMP

Translations of this manual into German, Italian and Spain are available on the project website: http://www.blendedlearning-quality.eu/

The price of the printed version only covers the printing costs (Amazon)

Disclaimer: This project has been funded with support from the European Commission. This publication reflects the views only of the BladEdu consortium, and the Commission cannot be held responsible for any use, which may be made of the information therein

Blended Learning Quality – Concepts Optimized for Adult Education

Editors
Peter Mazohl and Harald Makl (University of Technology Vienna, EIE/EBI Austria)

Co-authors
Peter Mazohl (EIE/EBI, Wiener Neustadt, Austria)
Harald Makl (EIE/EBI, Wiener Neustadt, Austria)
Luca Reitano (DigiLab University of Rome La Sapienza, Rome, Italy)
Michail Filioglou (EDRASE, Halki, Greece)
Nikolaos Tzimopoulos (EDRASE, Halki, Greece)
Felix Breitenecker (University of Technology Vienna, Vienna, Austria)
Andreas Körner (University of Technology Vienna, Vienna, Austria)
Stefanie Winkler (University of Technology Vienna, Vienna, Austria)
Pedro Luis Garrido Cano (SAFA Málaga, Spain)
Marco Moya Harrop (SAFA Málaga, Spain)
Ari Myllyviita (Viikki Teacher Training School of the University of Helsinki, Helsinki, Finland)

Published by

Printed by Amazon (Print on Demand)

About the Project

Blended Learning is a relatively new teaching method, which emerged in the last 8 years. Developed as a combination of classroom teaching and distance learning, this method takes up an important role in the educational system. Big companies were the first to use this teaching and training concept because they expected cost reductions. Nowadays the first research work about the efficiency and the necessary environment of Blended Learning are published. One of the issues mentioned is a missing quality concept for Blended Learning.

There exists the ISO/IEC 19796 norm (designed for distance learning) that could be more or less applicable for Blended Learning as well. As quality is beginning to play an increasingly important role in the educational system, the consortium extended the mentioned norms with a special focus on learners' needs. Additional, the consortium analysed and transferred the results of the research work dealing with Blended Learning into a quality framework for Blended Learning. The project focuses especially on the concepts of the quality of courses, the courses itself, the quality in organizations responsible for Blended Learning courses and activities, and last but not least on the needs and the environmental conditions of the learners. The result is a scientific bases – more or less theoretical – description of a practicable quality framework for Blended Learning, added by a course to teach the developed results. The consortium tested the course in a pilot environment (at the University of Helsinki). An equivalent course was hold with ten participants as a first trial in Wiener Neustadt by the EBI. Additional there was a compact eLearning course, based on a Moodle environment, developed.

The consortium's members are all involved in education or further education of adults and experienced in organizing courses for adults.

The result of the project is a well proofed practicable quality concept (in written form) covering all issues of Blended Learning with a special focus respecting the needs and the learning environment of learners as well. The quality concepts are developed for Adult Education in the frame of a Grundtvig Multilateral Project 539717-LLP-1-2013-1-IT-GRUNDTVIG-GMP. The versatile results of this project are also valid for Higher Education and in the VET sector too. The project results can easily be transferred to equivalent teaching environments in these other sectors of education.

Consortium Members - Contact

- ## DigiLab (University of Rome La Sapienza), Italy

Contact person	Luca Reitano
Web page	www.digilab.uniroma1.it
Email address	lucareitano@yahoo.it
City	Italy
Country	Rome

- ## Cultural Association – F.C. Europaclub, Italy

Contact person	Alberto Pigliacelli
Web page	www.europaclub.org
Email address	europaclub.pigliacelli@gmail.com
City	Rome
Country	Italy

- ## European Initiative for Education EBI/EIE, Austria

Contact person	Peter Mazohl
Web page	www.advanced-training.net
Email address	info@advanced-training.at
City	Wiener Neustadt
Country	Austria

- ## Educational Activities Society "EDRASE", Greece

Contact person	Michail Filioglou	
Web page	www.edrase.gr	
Email address	Evangelos Iliadis	vanil@otenet.gr
	Nikolaos Tzimopoulos	ntzimop@sch.gr
	Michail Filioglou	micfilioglou@hotmail.com
City	Halki, Dodecansese	
Country	Greece	

A guidance to Blended Learning

- ## University of Technology Vienna, Austria

Contact person	Prof. Felix Breitenecker
Web page	www.tuwien.ac.at
Email address	felix.breitenecker@tuwien.ac.at
City	Vienna
Country	Austria

- ## SAFA Escuelas Profesionales Sagrada Familia, Spain

Contact person	Pedro Luis Garrido Cano
Web page	www.safaicet.es
Email address	pgarrido@fundacionsafa.es
City	Málaga
Country	Spain

- ## University of Helsinki, Finland

Contact person	Ari Myllyviita
Web page	www.vink.helsinki.fi/
Email address	ari.myllyviita@helsinki.fi
City	Helsinki
Country	Finland

Chapter Overview

Chapter 1

"Our Understanding of Blended Learning" deals with the status of research in the frame of quality assurance in Blended Learning. Here the focus was laid on papers, documents and books describing the needs of learners.

Chapter 2

This chapter about "Quality Assurance in Blended Learning – a Quality Framework" summarises the findings of the consortium and presents a practicable quality framework with a special focus on the learners' needs

Chapter 3

The chapter about "Quality Criteria for the institution" gives an overview of quality criteria that should be used by the teaching institution before, during and after a Blended Learning course.

Chapter 4

In the chapter the "Enrolment in a Blended Learning course" is described from the point of view of a learner – what do learners expect, what do they need and how can a teaching organisation care for the necessary quality level?

Chapter 5

"The Course itself" is a big chapter including the results of the surveys performed during the project. These results give an overview about the technical issues of the eLearning Platform used in a Blended Learning course as well as the necessary tutorial support for the learners.

Chapter 6

"The Assessment" describes the normally final activity in the Blended Learning course and summarizes the expected quality assurance.

Chapter 7

In the chapter "The Pilot Course" - performed by the University of Helsinki - is described and the feedback of the participants is presented.

Chapter 1
Our Understanding of
Blended Learning

Authored by: Peter Mazohl (European Initiative for Education, Austria)
Luca Reitano (DigiLab Universitá La Sapienza, Italy)
Data collection: Kathrin Zehrfuchs
Final checks: Sophia Zolda
Language support: Sophia Zolda, Kathrin Zehrfuchs

Blended Learning does not only fit into the modern, connected lifestyle, but can also provide specific benefits to students, teachers and administration.[1]

---

[1] Ehlers, Ulf (2007) p 97

Contents of Chapter 1

1. The Term Blended Learning 13
   1.1. Various Definitions 13
   1.2. Our Understanding of Blended Learning 15
      1.2.1. Blended Learning as a teaching method 15
      1.2.2. Pedagogical access to Blended Learning 15
      1.2.3. Why Blended Learning? 16
   1.3. Blended Learning Environment 16
   1.4. The need of a quality framework in Blended Learning 17

List of Figures

Figure 1-1: Structure of Blended Learning (source: Mazohl 2015) 14
Figure 1-2: Blended Learning (source: Mazohl 2015, p 18) 15
Figure 1-3: Impacts to an optimised Blended Learning Environment 16

A guidance to Blended Learning

1. The Term Blended Learning

The term Blended Learning is generally applied to the practice of using both online and in-person learning experiences when teaching students (Abbott 2014). This term has developed for many years with changing interpretations.

Jane Hart (2015) ran a poll asking a unmentioned target group about their understanding of Blended Learning. She offered four different possible answers:

    A: A training programme containing a mix of face-to-face-and e-learning
    B: A training activity containing a range of formats and media
    C: A strategic L&D[2] approach to support a wide range of learning initiatives
    D: Other

The majority (of approximately 50 %) voted for answer A. The poll's results show on the other hand that there are different interpretations for Blended Learning and the term does not mean the same to all people.

1.1. Various Definitions

The term Blended Learning approximately exists since 2000. Donald Clarc (2003) gives an interesting statement about Blended Learning:

> *'What is 'blended learning'? It is the use of two or more distinct methods of training. This may include combinations such as: blending classroom instruction with online instruction, blending online instruction with access to a coach or faculty member, blending simulations with structured courses, blending on-the-job training with brown bag informal sessions, blending managerial coaching with e-learning activities.'*

Elliot Masie

From statements like that, a further development of the term can be watched during the last decade. Charles Graham mentions the term "Blended Learning" in the handbook of Blended Learning (Bonk 2006, p 3) and defines it as a buzzword in corporate and higher education. It is one of the terms used besides distributed learning, eLearning, open and flexible learning or hybrid learning. More or less, all these terms mean the same: Teaching is split into different parts taking place in different environments (Mazohl 2015, p. 9).

The University of Waterloo (The Centre for Teaching Excellence, 2014) defines Blended Learning shortly *"Blended courses integrate face-to-face and online learning. Online and classroom activities and course materials are selected to complement each other, to engage students and to achieve specified learning outcomes."*

The Queensland University of Technology (2011) finally offers a very up-to-date definition:

> *Blended Learning is a practical framework that can be used to encapsulate a range of effective approaches to learning and teaching. It encourages the use of contemporary technologies to enhance learning, and the development of flexible approaches to course design to enhance student engagement.*

---

[2] L&D: Learning and Development

The University of Western Sidney (2013) defines Blended Learning in the following way:

Blended learning at UWS refers to a strategic and systematic approach to combining times and modes of learning, integrating the best aspects of face-to-face and online interactions for each discipline, using appropriate ICTs.

The Clayton Christensen Institute (2015), a non-profit nonpartisan research institute and think tank, published several documents about Blended Learning. Their last definition is often cited in literature:

The definition of blended learning is a formal education program in which a student learns:

(1) *at least in part through online learning, with some element of student control over time, place, path, and/or pace;*

(2) *at least in part in a supervised brick-and-mortar location away from home;*

(3) *and the modalities along each student's learning path within a course or subject which are connected to provide an integrated learning experience.*

In summary, Blended Learning is described as a combination of face-to-face teaching and some kind of technology based teaching - in most cases realized as distance learning. The term eLearning – often used in the context of Blended Learning – persists diffuse and is not clearly defined anyway.

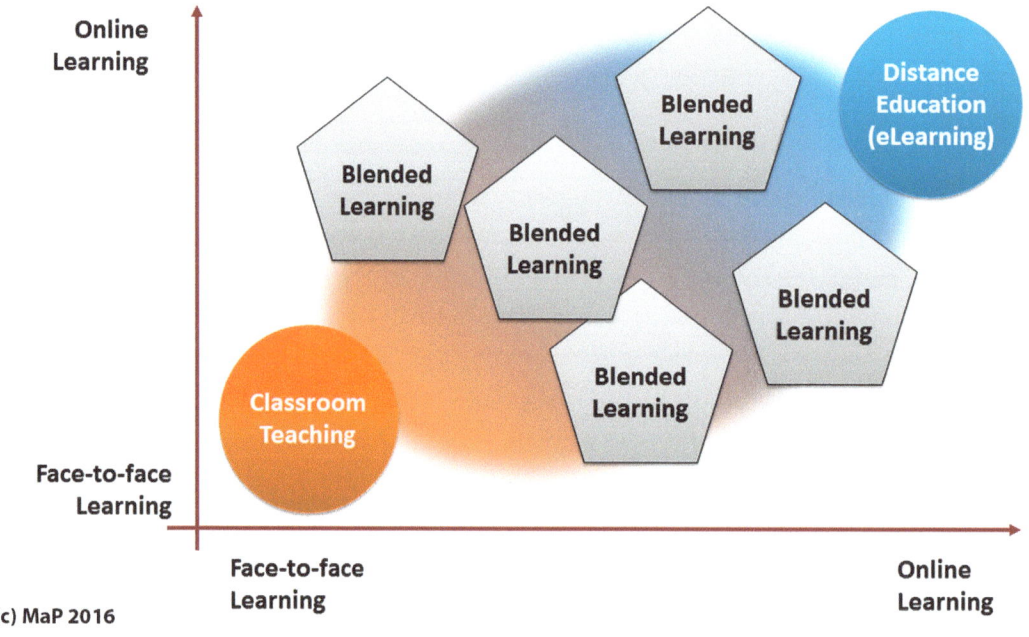

Figure 1-1: *Structure of Blended Learning (source: Mazohl 2015)*

Therefore, it is necessary to describe Blending Learning in the related context to clarify the starting position for all further discussions and descriptions.

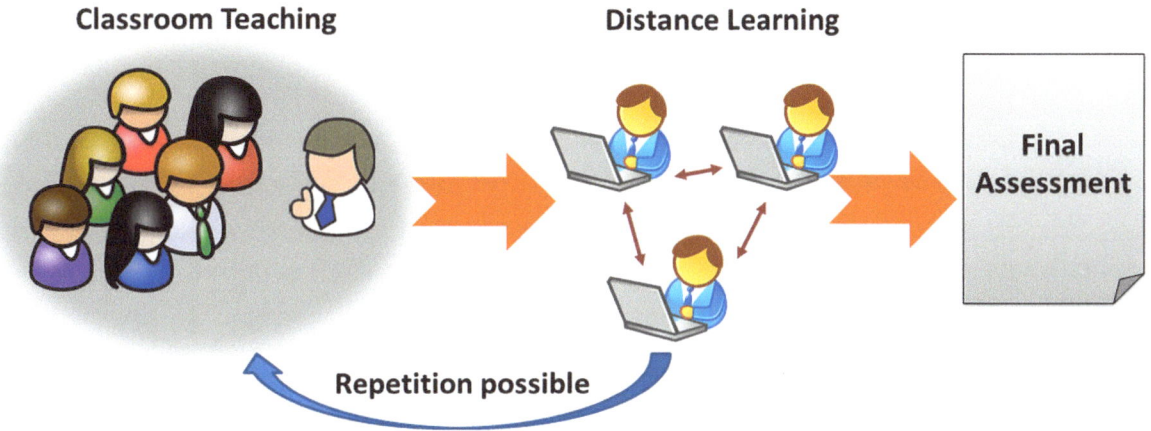

Figure 1-2: Blended Learning (source: Mazohl 2015, p 18)

There are many different other terms for Blended Learning: hybrid learning, technology-mediated instruction, web-enhanced instruction, mixed-method structure and others. These terms address more or less the same: a mixed method, consisting of minimum two different teaching modalities. Therefore, it is necessary to define the term "Blended Learning" in the used context to clarify what is really meant.

1.2. Our Understanding of Blended Learning

Blended Learning – from the point of view of the consortium – means a teaching method, where face-to-face teaching is combined with distance learning. The teaching process is supported by the use of an appropriate learning platform. The term eLearning in this document refers to the platform-supplied distance learning.

1.2.1. Blended Learning as a teaching method

Blended Learning is a teaching method and no pedagogical or didactical concept. Blended Learning describes the technique used for teaching. The consortium sees this kind of teaching highly connected with the use of ICT. ICTs offer new opportunities but also new challenges for both instructors and students (Redmond 2011). Teachers and trainers change their working place and reduce the time used in the traditional brick-and-mortar environment. Students get the independency to decide, what, where, when and how they learn during the distance learning.

1.2.2. Pedagogical access to Blended Learning

Teaching needs some pedagogical access. There are several different options for teachers. The consortium promotes a learner-centered access to Blended Learning because it fosters active learning, student engagement and involves the students more intensively in the learning process. Weimer (2012) mentions in her blog the advantages of learner-centered teaching (engagement of students, explicit skill instructions, reflection of students, motivation for students for self-control, encouragement for students to collaboration). The consortium recommends a student-centered access to Blended Learning for optimized results in teaching.

Another important issue is the description of the learning outcomes: The learning goals should be defined competence oriented. Therefore, it is possible to split the learning outcomes to the face-to-face teaching and the distance learning. This access is practically realized in the Blended Learning Project "AKMAT" which is currently running at the University of Technology Vienna (Breitenecker, 2014).

1.2.3. Why Blended Learning?

Obviously, Blended Learning aims to use the best combination from two different teaching methods. This leverage of the best aspects leads to better learning success, better knowledge or competences of the students and finally a higher level of students' satisfaction in learning. In the same way, the teaching success of the involved teachers (or trainers) increases. Kim (2016) predicted in her summary of studies an increasing development of distance learning and anticipated the current development towards Blended Learning.

1.3. Blended Learning Environment

Blended Learning can be seen as a learning environment compiled of various ingredients. Blended Learning per se means the method of teaching (combining face-to-face learning experience with distance learning). Blended Learning needs an appropriate set of components to work successfully in teaching. The ideal-case learning environment should provide an optimised teaching and learning climate, which is supportive, challenging, conducive to risk-taking and optimized to support the students. A possible (technical and pedagogical-based) learning environment in Blended Learning should take care of various issues and impacts:

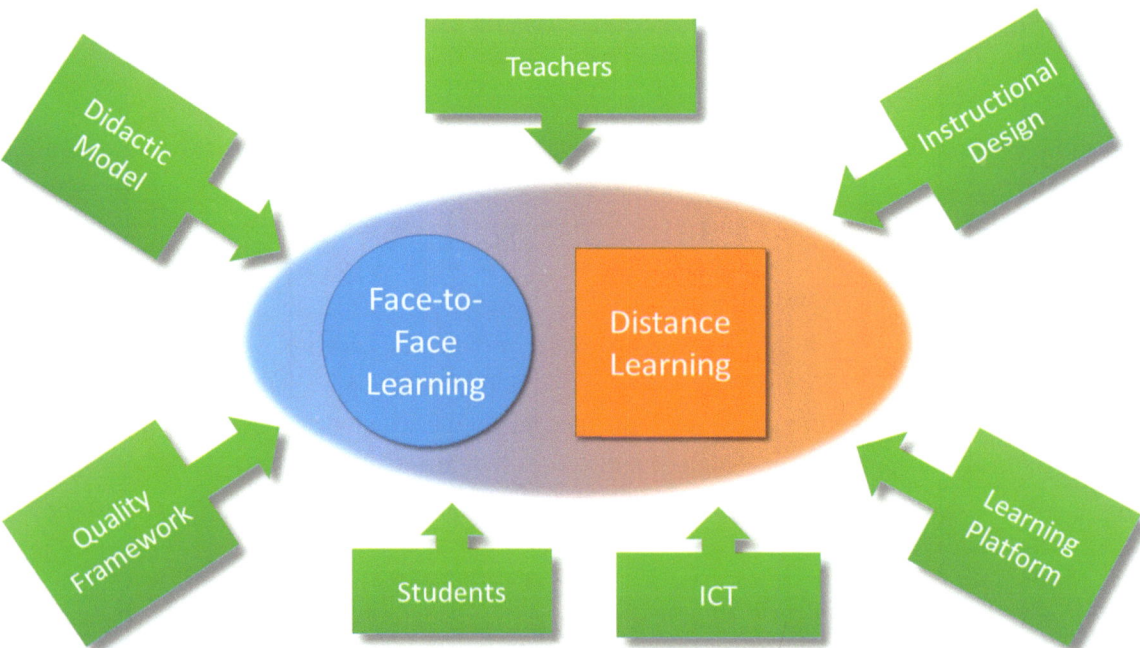

Figure 1-3: Impacts to an optimised Blended Learning Environment

The current project focuses on the definition of a possible quality framework to provide optimised quality in teaching for the learner. The source of the studies and developments in the project are focusing primarily on

Adult Education, but the framework can be used without modifications for VET learners and in Higher Education as well.

The transfer to school education does not seem to be very easy, because in many cases the youth of the learners are connected with some missing maturity in learning (Donelly 2010). That must be considered in using Blended Learning with younger students.

1.4. The need of a quality framework in Blended Learning

Ehlers (2007, p. 96) defines quality in eLearning and education as:

> *Quality in e-learning has become a leitmotiv in educational policies, an imperative for practitioners, and a huge demand for learners*

This is valid for Blended Learning as well. He mentions "Quality development in education is viewed as the result of quality competence of the involved stakeholders." The proposed quality framework considers all of that and focuses on the mentioned stakeholders: learners, teachers and institutions. Additional, other relevant factors were taken in account to provide a quality framework.

Sources

Abbott, S. (2014): *The glossary of education reform. Blended Learning Definition*. Available online at http://edglossary.org/blended-learning/, checked on 7/30/2015.

Bonk, Curtis Jay; Graham, Charles Ray (Eds.) (2006): *The handbook of blended learning. Global perspectives, local designs*. 1st ed. San Francisco: Pfeiffer (Pfeiffer essential resources for training and HR professionals).

Breitenecker, Felix; Körner, Andreas; Winkler, Stefanie (2014): *AKMATH. Institut für Analysis und Scientific Computing, UT Vienna*. Available online at http://akmath.tuwien.ac.at/, checked on 11/3/2014.

Christensen Institute (2015): *Blended Learning Definitions | Christensen Institute*. Available online at http://www.christenseninstitute.org/blended-learning-definitions-and-models/, checked on 7/31/2015.

Clarc, Donald (2003): *Blended Learning*. In *EPIC Whitepapers*. Available online at http://www.alapitvany.oktopusz.hu/domain9/files/modules/module15/261489EC2324A25.pdf, checked on 7/30/2015.

Donnelly, Roisin (2010): *The Nature of Complex Blends: Transformative Problem-Based Learning and Technology in Irish Higher Education*. In Yukiko Inoue (Ed.): Cases on online and blended learning technologies in higher education. Concepts and practices. Hershey PA: Information Science Reference.

Ehlers, Ulf (2007): *Quality Literacy — Competencies for Quality Development in Education and e-Learning*. In *Educational Technology & Society* 10 (2), pp. 96–108, checked on 4/21/2015.

Hart, Jane (2015): *What does the term "blended learning" mean? The results*. Available online at http://www.c4lpt.co.uk/blog/2015/01/25/what-does-the-term-blended-learning-mean-the-results/, checked on 7/30/2015.

Kim, Kyong-Jee; Bonk, Curtis J. (2006): *The Future of Online Teaching and Learning in Higher Education*: The Survey Says… In *EDUCAUSE Quarterly* 4. Available online at https://net.educause.edu/ir/library/pdf/EQM0644.pdf, checked on 8/1/2015.

Mazohl, Peter (2015): *Quality in Blended Learning. Concepts for a Quality Framework in Blended Learning*. Wiener Neustadt: Mazohl Publishing.

Queensland University of Technology (2011). *Protocols: Blended Learning*. Retrieved 11 June 2011 from http://www.ltu.qut.edu.au/curriculum/documents/PLC_blended_learning.pdf

Redmond, Petra (2011): From face-to-face teaching to online teaching - Pedagogical transitions. Available online at http://www.ascilite.org.au/conferences/hobart11/downloads/papers/Redmond-full.pdf, checked on 10/23/2014.

Saliba, Gina; Rankine, Lynnae; Cortez, Hermy (2013): *Fundamentals of Blended Learning. Learning and Teaching Unit 2013*. University of West Sidney. Sidney. Available online at http://www.uws.edu.au/__data/assets/pdf_file/0004/467095/Fundamentals_of_Blended_Learning.pdf, updated on 2013, checked on 1/25/2015.

The **Centre for Teaching Excellence** (Ed.) (2014): *Blended learning. University of Waterloo*. Available online at https://uwaterloo.ca/centre-for-teaching-excellence/resources/blended-learning, updated on 10/16/2014, checked on 10/16/2014.

Weimer, Maryellen (2012): *Five Characteristics of Learner-Centered Teaching*. Available online at http://www.facultyfocus.com/articles/effective-teaching-strategies/five-characteristics-of-learner-centered-teaching/, updated on 2/4/2015, checked on 2/4/2015.

Weimer, Maryellen (2013*): Learner-centered teaching. Five key changes to practice.* Second edition. San Francisco, CA: Jossey-Bass, A Wiley Imprint.

Chapter 2:
Quality Assurance in Blended Learning - a Quality Framework

Authored by: Peter Mazohl (European Initiative for Education, Austria)
Harald Makl (European Initiative for Education, Austria)
Data collection: Sophia Zolda, Kathrin Zehrfuchs
Final checks: Sylvia Mazohl
Language support: Kathrin Zehrfuchs

It is suggested that quality development is a constant negotiation process in which all stakeholders should participate in a common effort to define and implement quality in a continuous, improved way.[3]

---

[3] Ehlers, Ulf (2007) p 97

Contents of Chapter 2

2. Quality Assurance in Blended Learning – a Quality Framework 23
   2.1. Description of a versatile quality framework for blended learning 23
      2.1.1. Preconditions for quality frameworks 24
      2.1.2. The quality framework developed in the project 25
   2.2. Overview of the developed Quality fields 27
      2.2.1. Quality of the Institution 27
      2.2.2. Enrolment 28
      2.2.3. Course 29
      2.2.4. Learning Environment and Learning Phase 30
      2.2.5. Assessment and Evaluation 32
   2.3. Access to quality development in educational courses 33
   2.4. Sources 35

List of Figures

Figure 2-1: Three fields involved in the quality framework 24
Figure 2-2: Layer model (see: Varlamis, Apostolakis) 25
Figure 2-3: ISO process model (basic structure) 26
Figure 2-4: Defined quality fields as described in this paper 26
Figure 2-5: The institution's quality 28
Figure 2-6: The enrolment 29
Figure 2-7: The course itself 30
Figure 2-8: Issues and elements of the learning environment 32
Figure 2-9: Assessment and evaluation 33

List of Tables

Table 2-1: Common features in an LMS 32

2. Quality Assurance in Blended Learning – a Quality Framework

Blended learning enables the learner to learn and to study in a very special way. The teaching is split into on-site learning and distance-learning phases. In spite of the on-site teaching, which is regulated very strictly by time factors and the work in the group, the distance learning enables the learner to decide when, how and how fast to learn. (Stein, Graham, 2014)

The system seems to provide a lot of freedom to the learner (Deschacht; Goeman, 2015) – on the other hand, a learning success is expected from the learner. To evaluate the learning success an appropriate evaluation system is necessary. Using well-defined indicators does not make it difficult to find out the learner´s success (if the learner achieved a learning success).

The learner's success is only one special part in the teaching and the learning process. An overall system must exist to ensure the quality of the complete course. That makes it necessary to care for a certain level of quality assurance during the course. To provide this quality assurance a well-defined and embracing quality framework must exist.

Quality in teaching is an issue of increasing importance – for educational organisations as well as for learners. Quality normally is defined using standards. These standards only can be developed by authorized institutions, in Europe for example the ISO institution. These standards for blended learning are missing from the ISO norms. There exists the ISO/IEC[4] 19796 since 2005, but it is not completed yet. The ISO/IEC19696 provides a process model focusing on course providers including learners as well (Pawlowski 2007). The three main parts cover

1. The documentation of processes for the development and the implementation of a quality management system
2. The analyses of an existing quality management system and the evaluation focusing on amendments
3. Re-structuring of processes and organisational units to provide a change management

These ISO/IEC norms are the first international standards for quality management with a focus on eLearning (which is only one part of blended learning). These definitions provide a model that must be adapted to the teaching conditions of a specific teaching institution or course provider. The missing standards for the on-site teaching can be taken from other fitting ISO norms (for example from the ISO 900X family for educational organisations).

That causes the definition of a specific quality framework based on the described process model. The current project enhances the descriptions by a special versatile quality framework focusing on the learner's needs.

2.1. Description of a versatile quality framework for blended learning

Developing a new quality system in an organisation means that quality objectives and instruments are implemented for the core processes. For example, that covers analyses of learners´ needs, design of learning systems, providing tutor support or performing assessments.

The process model serves as a guide to specify those objectives. An organisation should go through the processes of the model and should answer the following questions for each process:

1. What is the main quality objective for a process?

---

[4] International Organization for Standardization / International Electrotechnical Commission

2. Who are the responsible actors?
3. Which methods or instruments can be used to assure quality?
4. How can we measure the success of the quality objective?

Pawlowsky (2007) mentions the possibility of the development of quality profiles for organisations including objectives, methods, relations and people involved. This matches to the proposal of the consortium.

The processes therefore just serve as a guideline to discuss quality and to set specific objectives in order to reach the best outcome or results.

2.1.1. Preconditions for quality frameworks

Quality educational programs begin with the development of quality courses. Quality courses either need standards for the quality assurance or a quality framework considering all necessary issues for an appropriate quality assessment (Chao 2003).

Pawlowsky (2007) mentions that the needs of users and their organisations should be the main emphasis of quality standards (and quality frameworks). He also mentions the awareness of teaching organisations, that quality is important, but the adequate instruments are missing to fulfil the needs and to meet requirements. Therefore, they cannot easily adopt quality approaches in their organisations.

The development of a quality framework for blended learning is extreme complex because there exist three main fields, which must be connected:

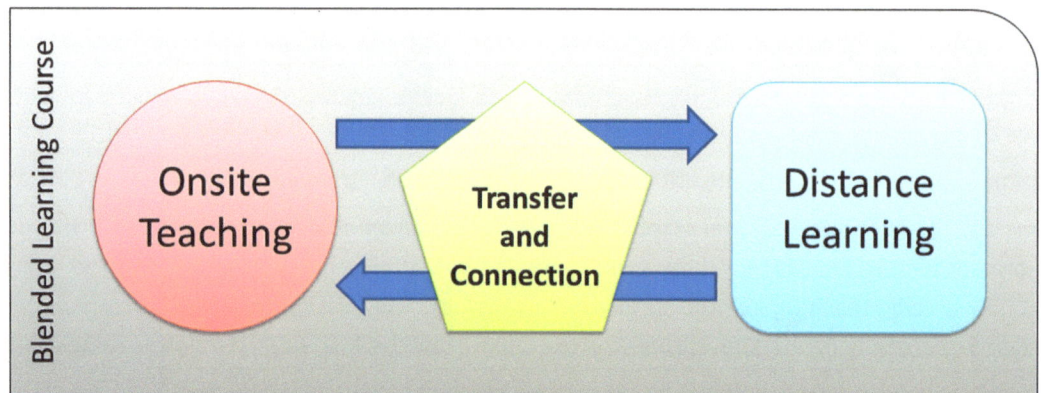

Figure 2-1: *Three fields involved in the quality framework*

- On-site teaching quality covers the quality of the teaching environment as well as the quality of organisation of the teaching and the other related typical on-site teaching issues.
- Distance learning quality focuses on the virtual learning environment (VLE), the provided material for students, the students' support, and other issues typically related to distance learning.
- Transfer and connection describes the methodology used to teach and assess the competence oriented learning outcomes. That means the methods to split the defined learning outcomes and dedicate partly to the distance learning or the on-site teaching.

Varlamis and Apostolakis (2010) define four layers for a typical blended learning course: the pedagogical layer, a technical layer, a social layer and finally an organisational axis. This model is based on evaluation criteria for learning systems.

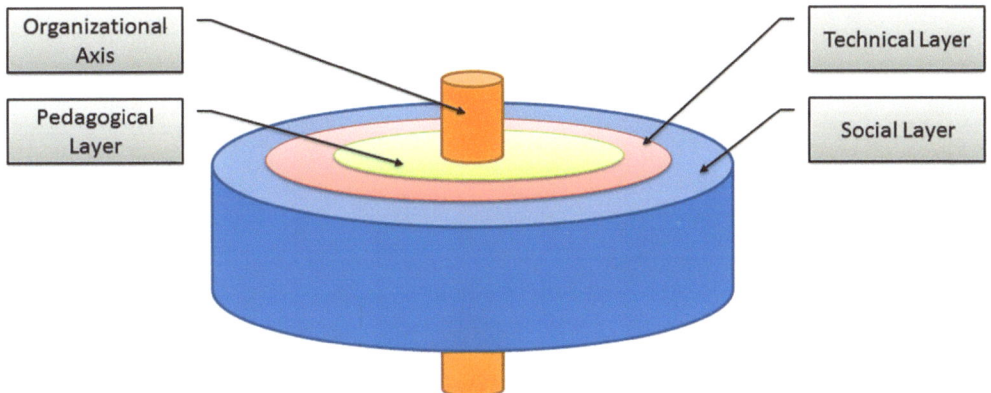

Figure 2-2: Layer model (see: Varlamis, Apostolakis)

- The pedagogical aspect covers the quality of the learning process (this can be evaluated by the reaching of the pedagogical targets). The pedagogical targets should be clear (and appropriate communicated) for all learners. Tutors are responsible for performing educational tasks (that implicates a well-defined tutorial support).
- The technical aspect means basically the infrastructure of the organisation.
- The social aspect addresses to a learning community. Learning (to reach the targets) is a kind of communal effort.
- The center of all learning and teaching activities is the organisation.

The mentioned model could be a solution to develop a quality framework; nevertheless, the access to the quality framework in the current project is focusing on the learners´ needs and not on course evaluation. Therefore, the project defines a quality framework based on the learner, the activities of the learner during the course, the environment of the learner and other issues in direct context with the learner. The requirements for the institutions are part of the framework as well as the necessary preconditions for teachers.

2.1.2. The quality framework developed in the project

The research work of the project defines a different model using the existing ISO/IEC 19796 to enhance the definitions with a focus on the learner as the center of the learning and teaching process.

The process model of the ISO/IEC is a guide for the development of learning scenarios (Pawlowsky 2007). The process itself is split into seven different parts. That are the

- Needs analysis, the
- Framework analysis, the
- Conception (or design), the
- Development (or production), the implementation, the

- Learning process, and finally the
- Evaluation (and optimization).

Mazohl (2015) gives a graphic overview of the process:

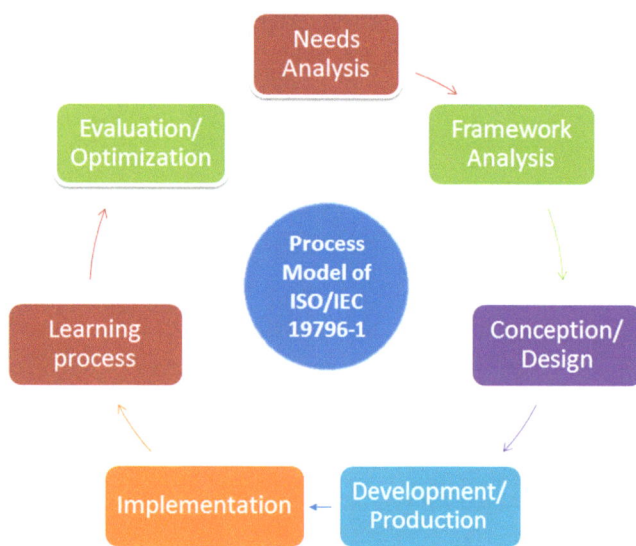

Figure 2-3: *ISO process model (basic structure)*

The goal of the ISO/IEC 19796-1 is to harmonize existing approaches to quality assurance. The description is on an abstract level. There do not exist neither recommendations nor guidelines for quality management. The user – in our case the course provider or providing institution – is responsible. These guidelines have to be developed by the institution/course provider itself (Pawlowski 2007).

The consortium gives recommendations, how the guidelines – based on the description of the abstract model – can be developed including the special focus on the learner's needs.

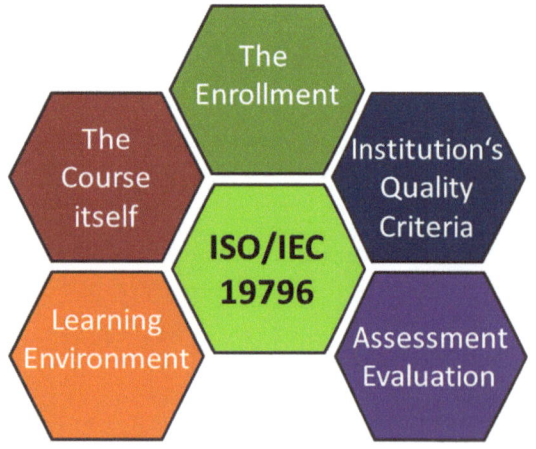

Figure 2-4: *Defined quality fields as described in this paper*

The consortium proposes to acknowledge that quality of a learning process is not something that is delivered to a learner by a course provider but rather constitutes a process of co-production between the learner and the learning-environment. The organisational aspects are mainly researched and the currently used standards (like ISO 900X) cover the quality fields of the course environment.

Ehlers (2008, p 21) gives a critical analyses of quality in the field of education and further education. He explains that quality in education is a multilayer issue and that it is represented in various models.

2.2. Overview of the developed Quality fields

2.2.1. Quality of the Institution

The learner has to trust the institution and to feel sure that the teaching institution will undertake everything to satisfy the learner's needs. Here is a list of different aspects (mainly regulated by ISO or similar norms) which are important for the learner.

- **Administration**
  - Technical Administration
    Students must be administrated well – that covers the procedure of the enrolment (including appropriate privacy measures) as well as all the administrational stuff during the course participation.
  - Program Administration
    The organisation cares for appropriate measures to announce the course, publish the content and all issues related to the course.

- **Documentation**
  The quality of documentation should cover the control of all documents, the change management, course descriptions, produced and published materials, reports and other related issues.

- **Resources** of the institution / Course provider
  - **Technical Resources**
    Varlamis and Apostolakis refer to the technical quality aspect in their study and mention the need of high quality of the used ICT as well as the used communication and learning platform (Varlamis, Apostolakis 2015, p 27).
  - **Human Resources**
    The human resources are the available staff in the course and the additional people involved in the course (for example administration).
  - **Financial Resources**
    The financial resources of the institution are necessary to ensure all learners to be able to finish the course in an appropriate way.

- **Teachers/Trainers**
  - **ICT Skills**
    ICT and the use of ICT is a crucial quality criterion in modern teaching. Van Lakerfeld (2011, p 10) mentions ICT as a necessary tool in adult education – that must be expended to all kind of education as well. Tilkin (2007, p 44 – 46) also mentions the need of ICT in teaching as an important issue.

- **Didactic Skills**

  Hénard and Roseveare (2012, p 17) explain in the report for the OECD that "there is evidence that participation and engagement in professional development activities are related to the quality of student learning." Obviously is that relevant for the didactic skills.

- **Instructional Design**

  Wright (2011, p 7) offers in his summary of quality criteria for evaluating the quality of online courses a list of instructional strategies, which can be used as a checklist for quality in teaching.

Figure 2-5: The institution's quality

2.2.2. Enrolment

Athiyaman (1997) describes the context of student's expectation and the student's satisfaction. In literature, the quality of enrolment is not described or mentioned. Therefore, the consortium developed guidelines for quality assurance in context with the enrolment based on the learners needs.

The enrolment contains two different items that are crucial for learners: information about the course and the practical handling of the enrolment.

- **Course information**
  - **Pre-Knowledge**
    A precise description of the necessary students´ pre-knowledge is an absolute quality criterion. The course provider must care for a well-described list of requirements for students.
  - **ICT Skills**
    The necessary ICT skills must be published in an appropriate way to the students. High quality institutions may offer special courses to take the students to the same (necessary minimum) level.
  - **Structure of the course**
    The timetable, estimated workload, assessment rules, and other course related issues must be published in a plain summary. Wright (2011) mentions that learners must be provided with general information about the course structure.
- **Enrolment procedure**
  - **Registration**
    The registration procedure must be defined properly; also, the various steps for the enrolment

must be defined suitably. Students have to get all the information in time in a plain description. Many big universities offer well-structured information and guide lines for their students and may work as an example of good practice.[5]

- o **Handling**
  The teaching organisation provides o policy with well-defined and clear processes for the learners during the enrolment.
- o **Access to software, materials, ...**
  This information is necessary to inform the learner from the beginning about the necessary tools and materials.

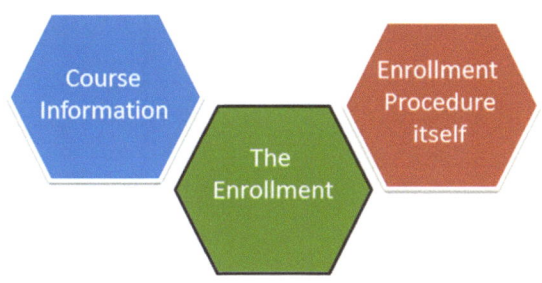

Figure 2-6: The enrolment

The literature research could not return any relevant results in context with quality and the course enrolment. The consortium presents the results of the Wiener Neustadt workshop in the Quality in Blended Learning Conference (2014) in this document. The findings need further investigation and should be topic of a broader study in the future (Mazohl, Peter (Hg.) 2014).

2.2.3. Course

The course quality can be seen from the course organisers' view as well as from the learners´. Jung and Latchem (2007) found that most institutions apply the same quality criteria for eLearning (and Blended Learning) as for the other modes of delivery. These criteria will satisfy the learner's needs only partially.

The workshop results defined the quality criteria for the course itself as follows:

- **Documentation**
  That covers the course documentation control, the description of the course, materials, and reports.
- **Get to know the tutor(s)/teacher(s) and the other learners**

---

[5] See: Registration Guidelines (2015). Available online at http://www.extension.harvard.edu/registration/registration-guidelines, updated on 3/6/2015, checked on 3/6/2015.

This special issue was mentioned by course participants of the EBI, but must be proved in further studies.

- **Well known course structure**
Wright (2011, p 6) describes a well-defined course structure as a quality criterion.

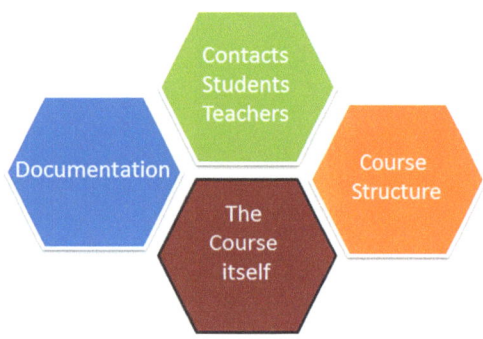

Figure 2-7: The course itself

2.2.4. Learning Environment and Learning Phase

In blended learning courses, the learning environment describes the face-to-face phase as well as the distance-learning phase. The UNESCO defines learning environment interestingly:

> *Learning takes place in multiple settings and the learning environment can be structured or unstructured and the learning in different environments can complement each other*
> (Wright, Clayton R. 2011, p 6)

Graham (2013, pp 8) identifies technology, ownership, definitions and seat time, incentives and evaluation as important issues in a blended learning environment.

The consortium identified various factors and issues of the teaching setting as an important quality criteria (Mazohl, Peter (Hg.) 2014). The listed items below are all focusing on the learners´ needs.

- **Teaching Activities**
Teaching activities should be conducted targeting to the learning outcomes, which should be defined as competence oriented learning outcomes as developed in the frame of LLP-Projects in Europe (van Lakerveld & Zoete 2011).

- **Distance Learning** (e-Learning)
Ehlers (2007) defines quality in eLearning as an imperative for practitioners, and a huge demand for learners.

- **Media**
The use of media is crucial in all learning environments, especially in the distance learning part of blended learning courses. Holden and Westfall mention, *"Media selection analysis must evaluate general and specific criteria, including instructional, student, and cost aspects for each delivery technology (or instructional medium) to ensure attainment of the instructional goal."* (Holden & Westfall 2009, pp 13)

- **Social Form** and Contact

  There are two important situations of interactions:
  - Interaction Students/Students
  - Interaction Students/Teachers

Besides the Learning Environment some other issues connected with the learner are to be considered.

- **Motivation**

  Students' motivation is a well-known success factor for learning and learning success. There exist many different studies about motivation but well-fitting motivation strategies are missing. An interesting access to motivate students is done by Chen and Jang (2010).

- **Workload**

  During the planning of the course it's necessary to estimate the students' workload in context with the learning and the necessary assignments. The strict planning of the course schedule must include security time gaps and learner-centered time schedules.

- **Communication**

  Mei-Jung Wang(2010) proves that – especially for students – the communication in the distance learning becomes crucial.

- **Technology**

  Blended learning is technology affected, especial ICT plays an important role. Amy Roche (2010, p 4) mentions the importance of the role of technology and that both students and teachers have to be comfortable with using technology (computers, software and internet).

- **Equipment** and **software**

  The used equipment must be state of the art and a well-fitting software must be available in the institution. If a special software is used the institution should offer the students special agreements to use this software for their assignments in distance learning.

- **Platform** for the distance learning phase

  To provide a high level of quality, the use of an eLearning platform is recommended (Aljawarneh, Muhsin & Nsour 2011). The platform used for the distance learning must fulfil a list of criteria.

  Stein and Graham (2014) give a simple definition of the common features in their book "Essentials for Blended Learning: A Standards-Based Guide":

Class Management	Communication and Interaction	Organization and Resources	Practice and Assessment
Class roster	Class announcements	Web page creation	Quizzes and tests
Grade book	Private messaging	Lesson sequencing	Surveys
Group management	Discussion forums	Outcome alignment	Online assignments
Peer review assignments	Live chat	File upload	Self-checks
Data tracking or learning analytics	Videoconferencing	Conditional release	Rubrics
	Multimedia comments	Collaborative editing	
	System notifications	RSS feed aggregation	
	Outgoing RSS feeds		

Table 2-1: Common features in an LMS

This description covers the basic requirements to an eLearning platform that can be used for Blended Learning.

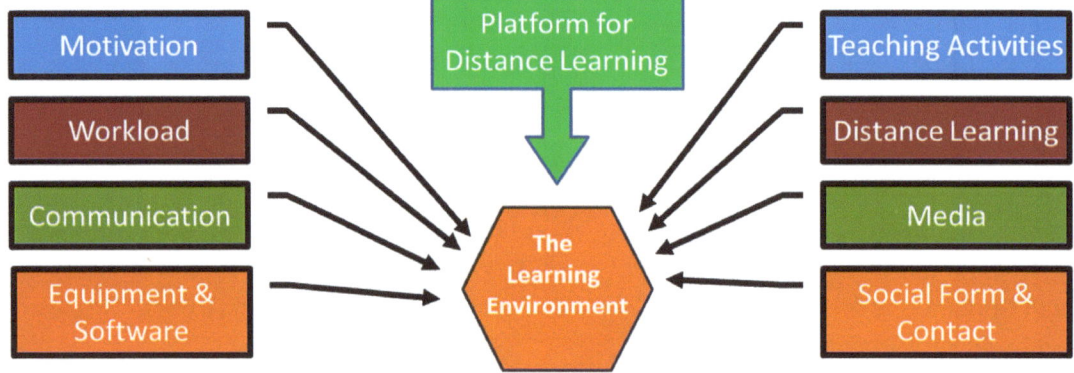

Figure 2-8: Issues and elements of the learning environment

2.2.5. Assessment and Evaluation

Assessments must be planned and defined before the course; the information about the assessments should be shared with the learner before the enrolment of the course (necessary pre-information). It could be useful to define a Learning agreement where times, tools, goals and duties (of learners and the learners´ employer[6] – if existing - are well explained from the beginning

---

[6] Not all learners are employed – there are freelancers or other people running their own business that are attending Blended Learning courses.

A guidance to Blended Learning

The assessment should be the closing element of a blended learning course, followed by the evaluation of the course (by the learner).

Two main criteria can be identified for the evaluation and assessment criteria fields:

- **Planning and definition of assessments**
  The assessment criteria must be published to the students at the begin of the course (or be published in the course description).
  The definition of the assessment must be done in the design and definition of the course.

- **Assessment execution**
  Assessments must be performed in a defined environment with properly defined assignments. A properly defined assessment should cover
    - The assessment's testing definition (what is going to be assessed in which way when and how)
    - The necessary description of the assessed competences or learning outcomes
    - A qualified evaluation of the assessment's results with fair feedback to the learners

- **Evaluation**
  The evaluation should cover
    - The evaluation of the course by the learners
    - The evaluation of the teachers/trainers (by the learners)
    - The evaluation of the course structure (in a defined quality management circle).

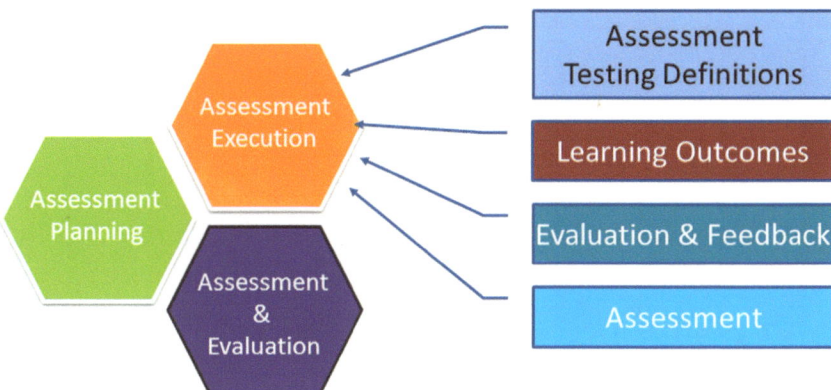

Figure 2-9: Assessment and evaluation

2.3. Access to quality development in educational courses

Ehlers (2008) mentions a list of different access methods to quality in teaching:

- Quality management (for example based on the ISO 9000:2000 standards)
- Evaluation techniques (for example self-evaluation) (Tilkin (Hg.) 2007, pp 8)
- Catalogues of criteria[7] or checklists
- Benchmarking (Ubachs (Ed.) 2012)

---

[7] The defined quality framework by the project's consortium is an enhancement of a simple criteria catalogue and covers more than simple checklists

- Accreditation and certification
- Seal of Quality

Sources

Aljawarneh, Shadi; **Muhsin**, Zahraa; **Nsour**, Ayman: *E-learning Tools and Technologies* in *Education: A Perspective* 2011.

Athiyaman, Adee (1997): *Linking student satisfaction and service quality perceptions*. In: *European Journal of Marketing* 31 (7), S. 528–540.

Bersin J. (2004). *The Blended Learning Book*. San Francisco; Pfeiffer.

Chao, Tracy (2003): *Establishing a Quality Review for Online Courses. A formal review of online courses measures, their quality in key areas and reveals changes needed for improvement*. In: *EDUCAUSE Quarterly* (3), S. 32–39.

Chen, Kuan-Chung; **Jang**, Syh-Jong (2010): *Motivation in online learning. Testing a model of self-determination theory*. In *Computers in Human Behavior* 26 (4), pp. 741–752. DOI: 10.1016/j.chb.2010.01.011.

Clark R.C. (2007): The *New Virtual Classroom*: Evidence-based Guidelines for Synchronous e-Learning, Pfeiffer.

Deschacht, Nick; Goeman, Katie (2015): *The effect of blended learning on course persistence and performance of adult learners: a difference-in-differences analysis*. In: *Computers & Education*.

Ehlers, Ulf (2007): *Quality Literacy — Competencies for Quality Development in Education and e-Learning*. In: *Educational Technology & Society* 10 (2), S. 96–108.

Ehlers, Ulf (2008): *Qualität und Bildung. Bedingungen bildungsbezogener Qualitätsentwicklung in der Aus- und Weiterbildung*. Universität Duisburg-Essen, Duisburg-Essen.

Eulers, D. (2005): e-*Learning in Hochschulen und Bildungszentren*, Band 1, Buchreihe e-Learning in Wirtschaft und Praxis, München, Wien, Oldenburg.

Graham, Charles R.; Woodfield, Wendy; Harrison, J. Buckley (2013): *A framework for institutional adoption and implementation of blended learning in higher education*. In: *The Internet and Higher Education* 18, S. 4–14. DOI: 10.1016/j.iheduc.2012.09.003.

Graham, Charles R.; Woodfield, Wendy; Harrison, J. Buckley (2013): *A framework for institutional adoption and implementation of blended learning in higher education*. In: *The Internet and Higher Education* 18, S. 4–14. DOI: 10.1016/j.iheduc.2012.09.003.

JISC (2006): *Effective Assessment for the assurance of academic quality and standards in higher education*; Gloucester.

Jung, Insung; Latchem, Colin (2007): *Assuring quality in Asian open and distance learning*. In: *Open Learning: The Journal of Open, Distance and e-Learning* 22 (3), S. 235–350.

Kirkpatrick D.L. & Kirkpatrick J.D. (2006): *Evaluating Training Programs. The Four Levels*. San Francisco; Berrett-Koehler Publishers.

Mazohl, Peter (2015): *Quality in Blended Learning*, Wiener Neustadt, Mazohl.

Mazohl, Peter (Hg.) (2014): *Quality issues for blended learning courses focusing on the learner*. Quality in Blended Learning. Wiener Neustadt, 20/02 - 22/02. EFQBL: BladEdu Consortium.

Ojstersek, N. (2009^2): *Betreuungskonzepte beim Blended Learning*. Münster/New York/München/Berlin Waxmann; 2009^2.

Pawlowski, Jan M. (2007): *The Quality Adaptation Model: Adaptation and Adoption of the Quality Standard ISO/IEC 19796-1 for Learning, Education, and Training*. In: *Educational Technology & Society* 10 (2), S. 3–16.

Stein, Jared; **Graham**, Charles R. (2014): *Essentials for blended learning. A standards-based guide*. New York: Routledge (Essentials of online learning series).

Tilkin, Guy (Hg.) (2007): *Self evaluation in adult Life Long Learning*. In coopperation with von Jaap Van Lakerveld, Selma van der Haar

Ubachs, George (Ed.) (2012): *Quality Assessment for E-learning: a Benchmarking Approach*. European Association of Distance Teaching Universities (EADTU). Heerlen.

Varlamis, S; **Apostolakis**, I (2010): *A Framework for the Quality Assurance of Blended E-Learning Communities*, KES 2010, Part III, LNAI 6278, pp. 23–32, Springer-Verlag Berlin Heidelberg;

Wang, Mei-jung (2010): *Online collaboration and offline interaction between students using asynchronous tools in blended learning*. In *Australasian Journal of Educational Technology* 26 (6). Available online at http://www.ascilite.org.au/ajet/ajet26/wang.html.

Wright, Clayton R.: *Criteria for Evaluating the Quality of Online Courses*. Grant MacEwan College, Edmonton, Canada. Instructional Media and Design.

Chapter 3:
Quality Criteria for the Institution

Authored by: Peter Mazohl (European Initiative for Education, Austria)
Harald Makl (European Initiative for Education, Austria)
Data collection: Sophia Zolda, Kathrin Zehrfuchs
Language support: Kathrin Zehrfuchs
Final checks: Kathrin Zehrfuchs, Sylvia Mazohl

Experience showed that fostering quality teaching is a multi-level endeavour.[8]

---

[8] Hénard and Roseveare (2012) p 7

Contents of Chapter 3

3. Quality Criteria for the institution 39
   3.1. Quality issues related to the Institution 39
      3.1.1. Administration 40
      3.1.2. Documentation 41
      3.1.3. Resources of the institution / Course provider 41
      3.1.4. Teachers/Trainers 42
      3.1.5. Instructional Design 43
   3.2. Other related issues 43
      3.2.1. Brick & Mortar environment 43
      3.2.2. Distance Learning 43
   3.3. Sources 44

List of Figures

Figure 3-1: The institution's quality 40
Figure 3-2: Resources of the institution and related quality criteria 41

List of Tables

Table 3-1: Statistic of students in UK 40

3. Quality Criteria for the institution

Students[9] have the right to get the best possible teaching environment and learning conditions in the frame of their education. That is valid for all learners, but especially in the context of HE[10], VET[11] and AE[12] using Blended Learning. It is expected that the teaching institution is interested in the learners' environment and cares for the needs of the learners.

Pitsoe and Maila (2014) mention that the concept "quality" often is used interchangeably with the concept of "quality assurance". Jung and Latchem (2007, p 237) mean that quality can have different meanings (for example for governments, employers, faculty members, and researchers). In this paper, we focus on quality criteria that can be used for quality assurance in a quality cycle with continuous amendments.

3.1. Quality issues related to the Institution

The learner has to trust the institution and to be sure that the teaching institution will undertake everything to satisfy the learner's needs. Here different aspects (mainly regulated by ISO or similar norms) are important for the learner. Quality issues and quality assurance are matters of growing interest in teaching institutions. That may be seen in context with a growing competition in the field of education but is mainly the result of a continuous development in increasing the quality in teaching in European countries.

Pitsoe and Maila (2014) describe that the question of quality is one of the most significant research areas – especial in ODL[13]. In most cases the research work focuses on the teaching itself of the environmental teaching and learning conditions. In almost no research studies the institution and the provided quality of the teaching institution is in the middle of the investigation or research work.

The consortium defined in a workshop at the conference about Quality in Blended Learning in Wiener Neustadt (Austria, spring 2014) a concept with several items closely related to the quality criteria necessary for the institution, mainly relevant for the pre-phases of a Blended Learning Course.

---

[9] In that paper, we address mainly to students and learners attending Blended Learning courses.
[10] Higher Education
[11] Vocational Education and Training
[12] Adult Education
[13] Open Distance Learning

Figure 3-1: The institution's quality

3.1.1. Administration

- **Technical Administration**

Students must be administrated well – that covers the procedure of the enrolment (including appropriate privacy measures) as well as all the administrational issues during the course participation.

An increasing challenge for many institutions is the increasing diversity of students. The reason may be from the raising share of young people enrolling in courses (for example in HE) with more mature students (Hénard, Roseveare 2012). Today, it is not unusual that students hold several master or bachelor degrees, are studying in a second subject as an amendment, or complement to their education (see Hénard & Roseveare, 2012, p 13).

The Hesa collects data about that issue in the United Kingdom[14].

	Percentage of HE students	
First degree	65,3%	
Postgraduate	22,9%	
Higher degree (research)		4,6%
Higher degree (taught)		13,1%
Other postgraduate		5,2%
Undergraduate	11,8%	

Table 3-1: Statistic of students in UK

In other European countries, the situation will be similar.

A special situation are VET courses, which focus on continuous education – here the students will be more inhomogeneous than these at HE level.

Appropriate methods, means and resources must be defined by the institution to administrate all the necessary issues correctly and with the necessary attitude dealing with privacy.

---

[14] HESA - Higher Education Statistics Agency (2015)

- **Program Administration**

    The organisation cares for appropriate measures to announce the course, publish the content and all issues related to the course. Shelton (2010) writes in the quality scoreboard about seventy quality indicators that administrators of education should examine in their quality assurance. The quality criteria should be defined in context to each institution in the framework (Shelton 2010).

    Possible items are the announcement of the course, the publishing, the correct planning of courses in well-fitting chains, or other related items.

3.1.2. Documentation

The documentation of the course is partly a result of the program administration, partly closely connected with the course. Documentation means a comprehensive, maybe an all-embracing description of all relevant issues in context with the promoted course.

The quality of documentation should cover the control of all documents, the change management, course descriptions, produced and published materials, reports, feedbacks and other related issues.

The University of Wales (University of Wales: Course Documentation, 2015), for example, provides a very detailed described system to provide the relevant description of the course. All the activities in course documentation lead to a student's handbook of the course, which is amended and updated in a well-defined process.

3.1.3. Resources of the institution / Course provider

Hénard & Roseveare (2012) list five areas where institutional policies work as an important impact in teaching: human resources; information and computing technology; learning environments; student support; and internationalisation. Human resources as well as the technology are items, which belong to the institution's quality.

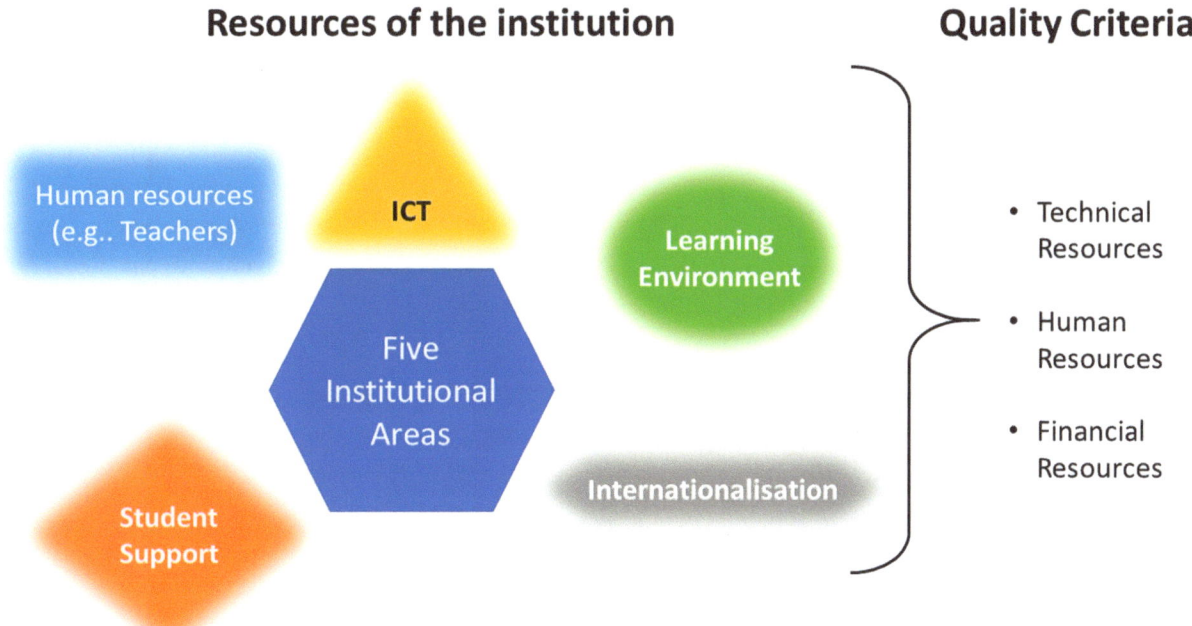

Figure 3-2: Resources of the institution and related quality criteria

A guidance to Blended Learning

- **Technical**

    Varlamis and Apostolakis (2015, p 27) refer to the technical quality aspect in their study and mention the need of high quality of the used ICT as well as the used communication and learning platform.

    The technical equipment – especial the ICT tools - need to be at the state of the art and supplied with well-defined and organised maintenance. All that technical infrastructure as well as the technical support should be planned at an institutional level (due to the costs) to ensure a high standard.

    The processes of planning should include an assessment of the added value or benefit of the use of technology in teaching as well as the exploration of the impacts of the introduction of technology into teaching and learning praxis (Hénard & Roseveare 2012).

    A special focus should be set on innovation. Innovation can be one of the main drivers of quality teaching improvement if it is supported at an institutional level. Hénard and Roseveare (2012) recommend to encourage teachers (and trainers) as well as students to be active innovators.

- **Human**

    The human resources are the available staff in the course and the additional people involved in the course (for example administration).

    Hénard and Roseveare mention, "there is evidence that participation and engagement in professional development activities are related to the quality of student learning (Hénard & Roseveare 2012, p 17)."

    The International Labour Organization defines a long list of issues related with teachers as important human resources in teaching (van Leur 2012). In that document the positive impact of continuous education to/of teachers – especial as In-Service training – is described and brought into context with the higher level of student's success in learning (van Leur 2012, p 75).

- **Financial**

    The financial resources of the institution are necessary to ensure all learners to be able to finish the course in an appropriate way. That covers the brick and mortar learning environment, tools, technical support and teacher's salary as well as the financing of the virtual learning environment.

3.1.4. Teachers/Trainers

Teachers must have the essential competences for teaching. This is required as well as to be effective in the classroom in the tutorial support as well as in online teaching (especially in Blended learning). This is one of the keys to raise levels of learners' attainment. Providing new teachers with initial teacher education of the highest quality, and encouraging serving teachers to continue developing and extending their competences throughout their careers, are both vital in a fast-changing world (Morisi 2013, p 4).

- **ICT Skills**

    ICT and the use of ICT is a crucial quality criterion in modern teaching. Van Lakerfeld mentions ICT as a necessary tool in adult education – that must be expended to all kind of education as well (van Lakerveld & Zoete 2011, p 10). Tilkin also mentions the need of ICT in teaching as an important issue (Tilkin (Ed.) 2007, p 44 – 46).

    The findings of the European Commission (DG Communications Networks, Content & Technology 2013) teach us that teachers and head teachers in Europe consider the insufficient ICT equipment to be the major obstacle to use ICT. In many European countries exists a lack of teachers who are well-educated in ICT (for example Luxembourg, Austria and Italy), therefore it is a must for institutions to provide

teachers with the necessary ICT skills, knowledge and experience (DG Communications Networks, Content & Technology 2013, p 55).

- **Didactic Skills**

Hénard and Roseveare (2012, p 17) explain in the report for the OECD that "there is evidence that participation and engagement in professional development activities are related to the quality of student learning." It is obvious that it is relevant for the didactic skills.

In all European countries, there exist a relevant further education for teachers and the teachers' training; this is also a relevant and important issue for the European Commission (Morisi 2013, p 6-7)

3.1.5. Instructional Design

Wright (2011, p 7) offers in his summary of quality criteria for evaluating the quality of online courses a list of instructional strategies, which can be used as a checklist for quality in teaching. Phipps and Merisotis (2000) recommend in their benchmarks guidelines regarding minimum standards for course development, design, and delivery. Learning outcomes - not the availability of existing technology - determine the technology being used to deliver course content. Especial in Blended Learning courses this is an important issue because it guides the course developer to distribute the learning outcomes to the onsite teaching or to the distance learning. In modern teaching the focus should not be set to learning outcomes only but also to a definition of the taught competences in the frame of learning outcomes (see van Lakerfeld and Zoete 2011).

3.2. Other related issues

It is a quality criterion of a teaching institution to care about the learner's needs. Beside the quality issues mentioned above the institution can provide additional issues (like material, information, examples) that helps the learner. In most cases, this will be necessary during the onsite teaching.

3.2.1. Brick & Mortar environment

Learners are accustomed to use their own equipment. In several European countries, for example in Austria, the use of laptops in teaching is usual (Sattler 2009). The learners need for an appropriate use of their equipment a well-structured electrical supply, the access to internet (by a free WiFi) with a sufficient bandwidth, fitting working places and other additional issues.

3.2.2. Distance Learning

The institution must offer the possibility that all students can use the learning platform with their equipment (Including tablets and mobile devices)[15]. That enforces the institution to survey the students regularly and to find out, if there are amendments and changes necessary.

---

[15] These requests were done by students of the UT Vienna Maths blended learning course and must be proofed by further studies. The focus round of the test course in Helsinki mentioned that issue as well.

3.3. Sources

DG Communications Networks, Content & Technology (2013): Survey of schools. ICT in education: benchmarking access, use and attitudes to technology in Europe's schools. Luxembourg: Publications Office. Available online at https://ec.europa.eu/digital-agenda/en/pillar-6-enhancing-digital-literacy-skills-and-inclusion.

Hénard, Fabrice; **Roseveare**, Deborah (2012): Fostering Quality Teaching in Higher Education: Policies and Practices. An IMHE Guide for Higher Education Institutions.

HESA - Higher Education Statistics Agency (2015). Available online at https://www.hesa.ac.uk/intros/stuintro1213, checked on 6/9/2015.

Jung, Insung; **Latchem**, Colin (2007): Assuring quality in Asian open and distance learning. In *Open Learning: The Journal of Open, Distance and e-Learning* 22 (3), pp. 235–350.

Morisi, Davide (2013): Supporting Teacher Educators for better learning outcomes. European Commission. Brussels.

Phipps, Ronald; **Merisotis**, Jaimie (2000): Benchmarks for Success in Internet-Based Distance Education. In *The Institute for Higher Education Policy*. Available online at http://www.ihep.org/research/publications/quality-line-benchmarks-success-internet-based-distance-education.

Pitsoe, Victor J.; **Maila**, Mago W. (2014): Quality and Quality Assurance in Open Distance Learning. In *Anthropologist* 18 (1), checked on 6/8/2015.

Sattler, Ruth (2009): eLearning im österreichischen Schulsystem. eLearning | Blended Learning | eTeaching. Vienna.

Shelton, Kaye (2010): A Quality Scorecard for the Administration of Online Education Programs | Online Learning Consortium, Inc. Available online at http://olc.onlinelearningconsortium.org/effective_practices/quality-scorecard-administration-online-education-programs, checked on 6/8/2015.

University of Wales: Course Documentation. Available online at http://www.wales.ac.uk/en/Registry/CollaborativeCentres/CourseDocumentation.aspx?tab=tab1, checked on 6/8/2015.

van **Lakerveld**, Jaap; **Zoete**, Joost de (2011): GINCO: Quality in courses. Quality features in the pre course phase; the development phase; the implementation phase, and the follow up phase of Grundtvig courses. PLATO.

van **Leur**, Alette (2012): Handbook of good human resource practices in the teaching profession. Geneva: ILO.

Chapter 4:
Quality Criteria for the Enrolment

Authored by: Peter Mazohl (European Initiative for Education, Austria)
              Harald Makl (European Initiative for Education, Austria)
Data collection: Sophia Zolda, Kathrin Zehrfuchs
Final checks: Sylvia Mazohl
Language support: Kathrin Zehrfuchs

Institutions need to ensure that the education they offer meets the expectations of students and the requirements of employers, both today and for the future.[16]

---

[16] Hénard and Roseveare (2012) p 3

Contents of Chapter 4

4. Enrolment in a blended learning course 47

    4.1. Importance of the decision 47

    4.2. The ideal learner for Blended Learning 47

    4.3. Quality criteria for the enrolment 48

    4.4. Sources 50

List of Figures

Figure 4-1: Some expectations from an "Ideal Blended Learner" 47

Figure 4-2: The enrolment 49

4. Enrolment in a Blended Learning course

4.1. Importance of the decision

Blended learning courses can be found in HE[17], VET[18] and AE[19]. Often further training or continuous education for adults is offered as a blended learning course. That is valid for IST-courses[20] as well.

Athiyaman (1997, p 529) describes the context of student's expectation and the student's satisfaction. In literature, the quality of enrolment is not described or mentioned. Therefore, the consortium developed guidelines for quality assurance in context with the enrolment based on the learners' needs.

4.2. The ideal learner for Blended Learning

The ideal learner in a blended learning course is self-motivated and computer-literate gifted. These learners love (academic) challenges and have the capacity for group work and cooperation. They are expected to work independently and consistently, communicate frequently with their instructors (especially in the distance learning), and maintain satisfactory progress. They are encouraged to develop their skills and are opened up for new ways of learning. Furthermore, they try to achieve the best possible results.

Tabor (2007) mentions also students' learning maturity and readiness for Blending Learning, which means the skill of independent learning.

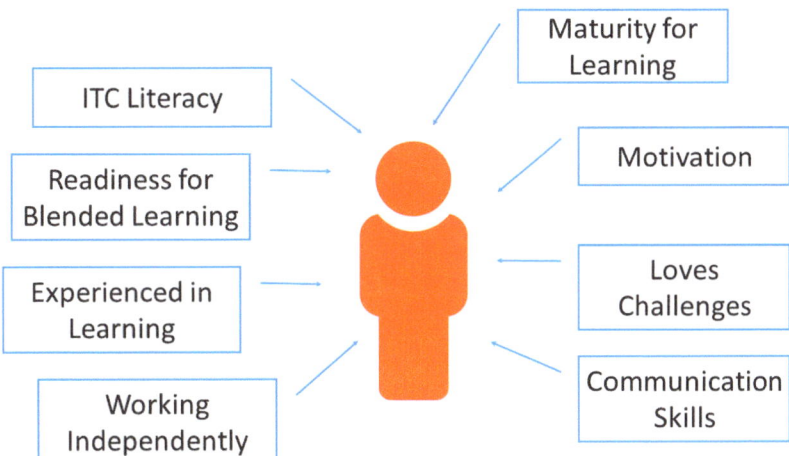

Figure 4-1: Some expectations from an "Ideal Blended Learner"[21]

All these skills should be present for a typical "blended learner" at a certain level. It is the responsibility of the institution to inform the learners about the frame conditions as well as the environmental conditions of the course. That covers all the issues expected from the learner during the course. Vaughan (2007) mentions that students have expectations that less face-to-face meetings means less work. Stacey (2008) proposes that

---

[17] Higher Education
[18] Vocational Education and Training
[19] Adult Education
[20] IST means In-Service Training
[21] Source: Peter Mazohl (2014)

A guidance to Blended Learning

"Consistent and transparent communication around the new expectations is needed in order to help students understand the blended learning process" (Stacey 2008, ascilite 2008 Melbourne). All that issues must be clear at the time the students enrol in the course.

4.3. Quality criteria for the enrolment

The enrolment contains two different items, which are crucial for learners: information about the course and the practical handling of the enrolment.

- **Course information**

    The start point for quality in the course enrolment is a complete and all-embracing course information. That covers mainly three issues:

    - **Pre-Knowledge**

        A precise description of the necessary student's pre-knowledge is an absolute quality criterion. The course provider must care for a well-described list of requirements for students. Kweldju (2014 p 72) mentions that studies from McKenzie & Schweitzer proofed a significant context between pre-knowledge and learning success.

    - **ICT skills and used software**

        The necessary ICT skills must be published in an appropriate way to the students. It is necessary to tell the students how and where the list is published.

        High quality institutions may offer special courses to bring the students to the same (necessary minimum) level.

    - **Structure of the course**

        The timetable, estimated workload, assessment rules, and other course related issues must be published in a plain summary. Wright (2011, pp 1) mentions that learners must be provided with general information about the course structure.

- **Enrolment procedure**

    - **Registration**

        The registration procedure must be defined properly; also, the various steps for the enrolment must be defined suitably. Students have to get all the information in time in a plain description. Many big universities offer well-structured information and guide lines for their students and may work as an example of good practice.[22]

    - **Handling**

        The teaching organisation provides a policy with well-defined and clear processes for the learners during the enrolment.

    - **Access to software and materials**

        At the beginning, it must be clear for the learners which software is used, how materials can be accessed, how they can get in contact with other participants, whom they can ask in cases of any problems or questions and other organisational issues directly connected with the learning

---

[22] See: Registration Guidelines (2015). Available online at http://www.extension.harvard.edu/registration/registration-guidelines, updated on 3/6/2015, checked on 3/6/2015.

processes, especial with learning in the distance phase. It also must be clear if there is any financial effort for the students.

The enrolment quality is closely connected with the course information and the policy of the institution. In a well-developed quality framework the teaching institution has to care for all the items mentioned in the first three chapters.

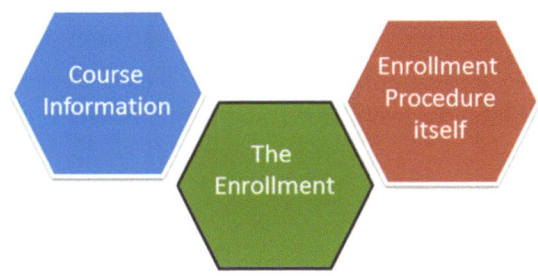

Figure 4-2: *The enrolment*

The literature research could not return any relevant results in context with quality and the course enrolment. The consortium presents the results of the Wiener Neustadt workshop at the Quality in Blended Learning Conference (2014). The findings need further investigation and should be topic of a broader study in the future (Mazohl (Hg.) 2014).

4.4. Sources

Athiyaman, Adee (1997): Linking student satisfaction and service quality perceptions: the case of university education. In *European Journal of Marketing* 31 (7)

Kweldju, Alex de (2014): Blended Learning Approach for Students With Low Prior Knowledge. In *Istech Journal of information media of science and technology* 6 (2), checked on 6/11/2015.

Mazohl, Peter (Ed.) (2014): Quality issues for blended learning courses focusing on the learner. Quality in Blended Learning. Wiener Neustadt, 20/02 - 22/02. EFQBL: BladEdu Consortium.

Stacey, Elizabeth; **Gerbic**, Philippa: Success factors for blended learning. In: Ascilite 2008 Melbourne, p. 5.

Tabor, Sharon W. (2007): Narrowing the Distance. Implementing a Hybrid Learning Model for Information Security Education. In *The Quarterly Review of Distance Education* 8 (1), pp. 47–57. Available online at http://robinwofford.wiki.westga.edu/file/view/24958021.pdf/238607251/24958021.pdf, checked on 8/6/2014.

Vaughan, N. (2007). Perspectives on blended learning in higher education. *International Journal on ELearning*, 6(1), 81-94.

Wright, Clayton R. (2011): Criteria for Evaluating the Quality of Online Courses. Grant MacEwan College, Edmonton, Canada. Instructional Media and Design.

Chapter 5:
The course itself

Authored by: Michail Filioglou
Nikolaos Tzimopoulos

Felix Breitenecker
Andreas Körner
Stefanie Winkler

Pedro Luis Garrido Cano
Marco Moya Harrop

Language correction and Final check:
Akrivi Anagnostaki

I know one thing: that I know nothing.[23]

I'm getting older while being taught all the time.[24]

---

[23] Socrates (5th century b.c.)

[24] Solon (6th century b.c.)

Contents of Chapter 5

5. The Course itself 55
   5.1. Organization of the course (On-site and on-line teaching) 55
      5.1.1. CMS course structure 56
      5.1.2. eLearning Platform 57
      5.1.3. Personnel Requirements 57
   5.2. Requirements of a Learning Platform 58
      5.2.1. Pedagogical Aspects 60
      5.2.2. Technical Aspects 63
   5.3. Students' Expectation of an e-learning Platform 66
      5.3.1. Trainees' needs 66
      5.3.2. Project evaluation on trainees' needs. 68
   5.4. Quality Criteria for a Blended Learning Platform 77
      5.4.1. Introduction 77
      5.4.2. Definitions 78
      5.4.3. Proposed Quality criteria 80
   5.5. Tutorial Support for the Online Teaching 81
      5.5.1. What students expect from the course tutorial support 81
      5.5.2. Quality criteria to support students 89
   5.6. Sources 91

List of Figures

Figure 5-1: Different aspects of Blended Learning... 55
Figure 5-2: CMS structure of the refresher 57
Figure 5-3: Typical BBS 59
Figure 5-4: SAFA Moodle... 60
Figure 5-5: Course Development 62
Figure 5-6: Motivation 62
Figure 5-7: Analyses of the learning tools (Boneu 2007) 64
Figure 5-8: LMS Evolution (1997-2010) delta Initiative 65
Figure 5-9: Importance of clear instructions.. 70
Figure 5-10: Ease of use of the platform and support 70
Figure 5-11: face-to-face and virtual activities covered by the platform 71
Figure 5-12: Importance of personalization... 71
Figure 5-13: Importance of only ONE platform including most of the activities 72
Figure 5-14: Answers of the sixth question with a mean... 72
Figure 5-15: The importance of one-to-one messaging tools between students................ 72
Figure 5-16: The importance of gamification inside the platform. 73
Figure 5-17: Importance of an existing connection to external social media....................... 73
Figure 5-18: Importance of group management of the platform 74
Figure 5-19: Learners can customize the platform to adapt it better to their needs. 74
Figure 5-20: Importance of an interactive way.. 75
Figure 5-21: Importance to find material easily 75
Figure 5-22: Importance of innovations at the platform. 75
Figure 5-23: The importance of interaction with their tutors.. 76
Figure 5-24: Learning with Tech trends 77
Figure 5-25: The course improvement process 78
Figure 5-26: LMS dependencies in Blended Learning (Source: Gaul 2014) 79
Figure 5-27: The number different ranges of age and number of questionees................... 82
Figure 5-28: The importance of direct contact with the tutor... 83
Figure 5-29: The importance of tutor contact.. 83
Figure 5-30: The importance of the instructional activities 84
Figure 5-31: The fourth question deals with different tools to contact instructors. 84
Figure 5-32: The fifth question asks about the availability of assignments......................... 85
Figure 5-33: The sixth question asks if a regular summary is necessary.............................. 85
Figure 5-34: The seventh question deals with the course progress 86
Figure 5-35: In the eighth question time restricted assignments are of interest. 86

Figure 5-36: In the ninth question different educational materials are discussed. 87

Figure 5-37: The tenth question asks about education goals. 87

Figure 5-38: The eleventh question deals with multimedia materials for educational purpose. 88

Figure 5-39: In the twelfth question, the learners decide if self-assessment is necessary. 88

Figure 5-40: The thirteenth question asks if learners want a visualization of their progress. 88

Figure 5-41: Replies about the importance of effort comparison 89

List of Tables

Table 5-1: Minimum requirements for LMS. 64

Table 5-2: The main problems encountered by trainees. 66

Table 5-3: General remarks of the trainers concerning a blended learning course 66

Table 5-4: Trainers' opinion. (Adapted: Nikolaos Tzimopoulos,2013) 67

Table 5-5: Review of Learners' needs 68

Table 5-6: Overview of the origins of all learners. 68

Table 5-7: Overview of the origins of learners' participation a survey about tutorial support. 81

5. The Course itself

The term "Blended Learning" is often used interchangeably in research literature along with "hybrid", "technology-mediated instruction", "web-enhanced instruction" and "mixed-mode instruction". Even though the concept of blended learning has been used for a long time, its terminology was not firmly established until around the beginning of the 21st century. The meaning of blended learning widely diverged to encompass a wide variety of synthesis in learning methods until 2006. Back then, the first Handbook of Blended Learning by Bonk and Graham was published. Graham challenged the breadth and ambiguity of the term's definition, and defined 'blended learning systems' as learning systems that "combine face-to-face instruction with computer mediated instruction" (Bonk, C.J., & Graham, C.R. (2006). P 5). Currently, the usage of the term Blended Learning mostly involves "combining Internet and digital media with established classroom forms that require the physical co-presence of teachers and students" (Friesen 2012).

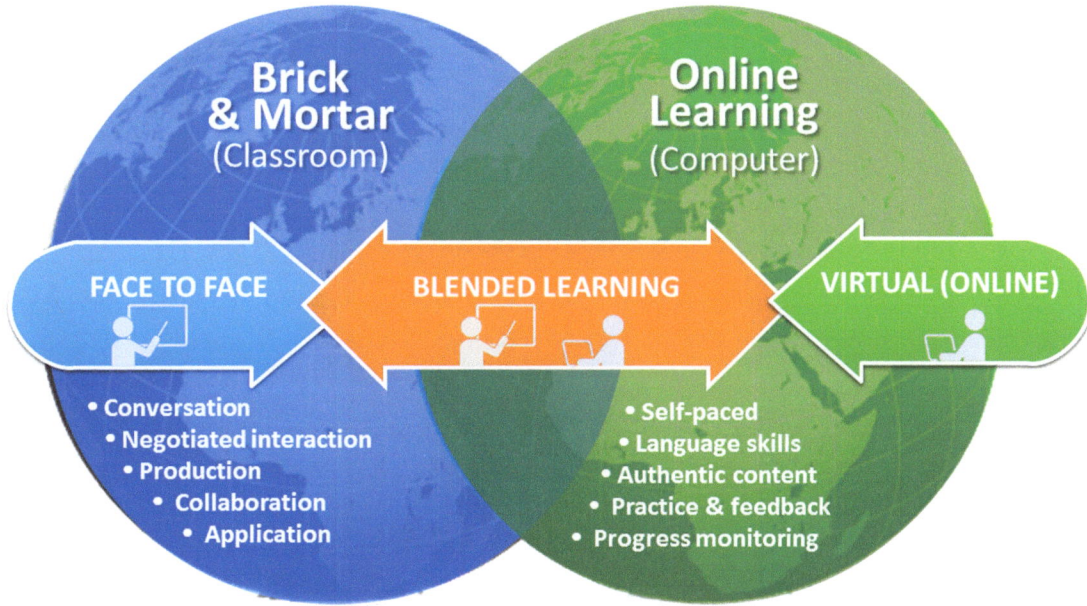

Figure 5-1: *Different aspects of Blended Learning[25] (Graphics: Peter Mazohl, 2016):*

5.1. Organization of the course (On-site and on-line teaching)

In 2008 the vice rector for academic affairs at the University of Technology in Vienna issued a project implementing a blended learning course for refreshing mathematical basic skills at the beginning of the study. The blended learning structure is applied on a course containing of lecture and exercise. It offers a more intensive facility for exercising and training of mathematical skills including formula manipulation and computation. The basic structure is fixed and consists of three parts:

- Lecture for introduction of the thematically field in the lecture hall.
- Exercise in smaller groups to practice examples and get familiar with the eLearning platform

---

[25] Retrieved from: http://www.theteslaacademy.com/whatisblended/

- Individual learning phase in self-organization in the eLearning system for exercising, testing and assessment.

Furthermore, the course has to be finished within 3 weeks so the design and organization is like an intensive course.

The module organization is thematically oriented to enable students a partial participation. The course administration regarding student registration and thematic setup is realized using a Moodle course. The Moodle course offers a framework fulfilling several requirements:

- User administration: register, contact, handling of certificates
- Material distribution: lecture notes, introductive examples, additional documents
- Exercise handling: connection to external server, administration of test results

One fundamental pillar of the course is the skill training of the students. This is not only within their responsibility also the lecturers guide the students using both platforms.

5.1.1. CMS course structure

The Moodle course has module structure, which is oriented on the thematically fields addressed in the course. Furthermore, the course integrates organizational and administrative issues like a time schedule, information about lecture halls and seminar rooms. The time schedule is an integrated external calendar, which can be downloaded to students' smartphones, tablets or notebooks.

The CMS course realized in Moodle enables students to contact the course responsible lecturers. In case of unexpected modifications, the organizer can also inform about changes in the schedule or other additional events.

The structural design of the Moodle course is illustrated in Figure 1. The header and the control section are predefined but some properties can be adapted. Despite of this the administrative information, the schedule and all the modules are user defined according to the different fields of studies and group of students. The structure has to be developed before the course starts. Nobody should start the course and design the structure on the fly parallel to the running course. The structure has to be defined before the course starts. Additionally, most of the content should be created and edited in advance. In the case of Moodle, this predefined materials and modules can be hidden until needed. Due to this fact the learning process is guided passively through showing particular content at the right time. If the structure is not predefined the effect of reworking afterwards would break the continuous flow of the guidance in the course.

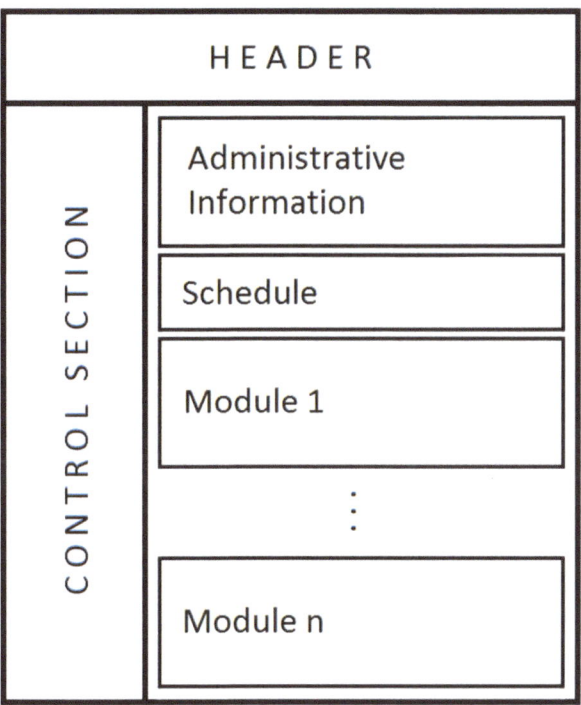

Figure 5-2: *CMS structure of the refresher*

5.1.2. eLearning Platform

In several fields of application, a simple CMS is not enough to fulfil all requirements of education. Especially in STEM subjects, often external applications are needed to offer required features. In case of Vienna UT an online mathematical training, testing and assessment platform was added. This platform should not be separated from the used CMS because than students will get confused in the learning process which will lead to frustration. Therefore, additional used tools should be somehow integrated in one system. There must be a clear structure, which can be followed by the learners. Exactly this scenario is present at Vienna UT. The additional mathematical practice environment Maple T.A., which is a powerful Computer Algebra System with an assessment interface, is directly connected to the Moodle based course webpage.

Each external platform has to be integrated in the existing environment in order to create a moderated platform guaranteeing a good basis for the blended learning course. Several components can be used, starting with at least a messaging system for distributing information to students up to forums and chats. If the aspects in forum or chat are also content related a moderation of this communication tool should be provided. All requirements learning platforms should fulfil are discussed in section 5.2.

5.1.3. Personnel Requirements

It is not enough to provide a well-designed blended learning course using a CMS and adding perhaps different online tools. An important part is the organization of useful face-to-face meetings. In case of the course at Vienna UT the former course consisted of traditional teaching approaches based on direct instruction or lecturing. Choosing a blended-learning structure requires several changes. Although the lecturing part could remain, the lectures and tutors have to modify their methods.

Producing printed manuscripts is not up to date anymore. Most of the materials are provided in some sort of online format. Lectures have to separate from old habits in order to offer an appropriate online format. In the case of Vienna UT, both lectures edited their lecture notes and offered them partly on the CMS. Due to the fact that most lecturers have many different courses if possible another party could administrate the CMS content in order to overlook the development of lecture and additional exercises.

5.2. Requirements of a Learning Platform

Before looking at the pedagogical and technical aspects of an LMS, we have to look at its origin and therefore its functionality.

The earliest forms of this type of education that we can call "correspondence courses" began with language classes in Berlin in the 1850s, although its real boom started in 1873 when the "Society to Encourage Studies at Home" was established in Boston. This gave students who could not attend or could not perform regulated studies the opportunity to receive instructions at home.

The way it worked was relatively easy. Students were contacted by e-mail by their tutor and received the necessary materials to develop the units that comprised the curriculum material. One of the primary needs of the LMS systems come from here and is called, the tutorial contact.

With the support of submitted materials (texts, videos, cassettes, etc.), students returned practical exercises for review in the same way. At that point, we could highlight other needs: the materials.

There were cases in which students went to the institution in person to attend tutorials, conduct examinations, receive clarifications or ask questions. And so the **activities** emerged.

Once the technology began to develop and It was accessible to students, we can see that the courses began to be taught through the radio and students could communicate with their tutor by phone. Therefore, we see that the **technical means** were incorporated into this type of education, becoming an indispensable medium. There are still many educational systems that use this medium[26].

With the arrival of the Internet, we find the first rudimentary attempts to "modernize" the above "correspondence courses" which would eventually change its name to "distance learning". In these early stages, the first elements were replaced (postal mail and telephone) to e-mails and mailing lists.

Only now, begin to appear the first "organized" systems such as Bulletin Board System or BBS. Bulletin Board System is a software for computer networks that allow users to connect to the system (via the Internet or through a telephone line) and using a terminal (Telnet program) which perform functions such as downloading software and data, read the news, exchanging messages with other users, playing games online, reading newsletters, etc.

---

[26]ECCA Radio in Spain. http://www.radioecca.org

Figure 5-3: Typical BBS (Source: Wikipedia[27])

Bulletin boards are in many ways a precursor of the modern forums and other aspects of the Internet. Historically it is considered that Ward Christensen created the first BBS software in 1978, whereas Usenet did not begin to run until the following year[28].

With the expansion of the Internet the first Content Management Systems (CMS) appeared, creating all kinds of activities (websites, forums, design, etc.), which later on, introduced the concept of "distance learning" with the result of the creation of specific learning CMS.

Of all the systems, Moodle[29] was highlighted because it grouped all the needs, which we have spoken about before and even more needs that have appeared later[30].

---

[27] https://de.wikipedia.org/wiki/Mailbox_%28Computer%29
[28] https://en.wikipedia.org/wiki/Bulletin_board_system
[29] https://docs.moodle.org/25/en/History
[30] https://docs.moodle.org/29/en/Main_page

Figure 5-4: SAFA Moodle

5.2.1. Pedagogical Aspects

The pedagogical aspect is the cornerstone of any educational structure. SAFA addresses multiple methodologies and training systems because of their wide range of training and diversity of contexts in the country. Therefore, we must make a distinction between two types of teachings that the institution now performs: **Formal education and informal education.**

"Formal education" comprises a set of teachings found within the Educational System, being regulated and organized by the Educational Administration, where a full valid academic or official title can be obtained. On the other hand, "non-formal education" offers greater freedom to develop varied educational plans and includes those teachings, lessons, courses, seminars ... on various topics that are made for beginners, specialize or to expand knowledge.

Given the importance that rests in the first group and the theme of this project, this section will focus on the characteristic that requires a training process of official e-learning courses, and SAFA requires.

The e-learning training has specialized for over the years, entering the field of formal education. This educational movement has matured reaching a balance between content and methodology used with the objectives and results with students. In this type of training, SAFA generally attends to the following profiles of students, above 25 years of age:

- Unemployed people looking to re-join the labour market.
- Employed people looking for new employment opportunities.
- Employed people who are looking to specialize or update their skills in their current labour activity.
- People who wish to obtain a curriculum with greater competences and abilities.

Given these profiles and possible family responsibilities or liabilities that they may have, the students' paces of work are very diverse. It is for this reason that the courses are structured in modules for easy adjustment to the students.

The standard **processes map** of an e-learning training course has the following structure:

1. Welcome meeting: Presentations by professors and students.

2. Basic platform operation: video conference room...

3. General course summary.

- Features
    - Official degree
    - Modular offer: training routes.
    - Validating subjects.
    - Learning tools for Tele-training.
    - Flexible hours: adaptability.
- Teacher training
- Resources
    - Tele-training platform (e.g. Moodle)
    - Corporative E-mail
        - E-mail
        - Video chat
        - Cloud documents
    - Videoconference (e.g. Blackboard Collaborate)

4. Presentation course. Practical aspects

- How the cycle develops?
- How to overcome the modules?
- Attendance exams
- Performing tasks
- Forum use and functions

5. Questions and answers

Course Development

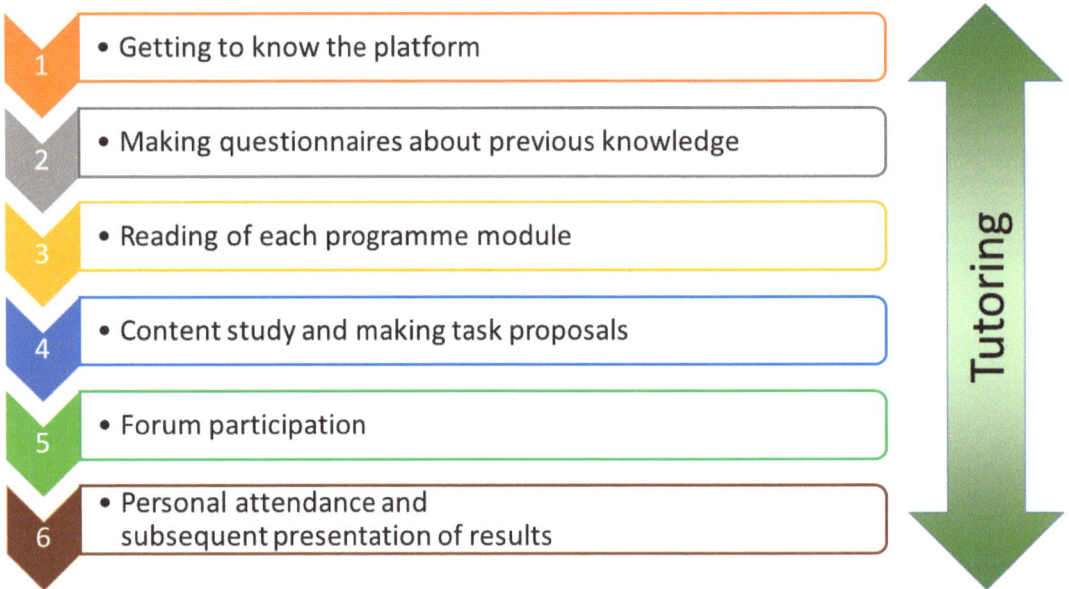

Figure 5-5: Course Development

On the other hand, the main driving force of eLearning is the **motivation** of each person. You can offer quality content in the eLearning courses, but it is uncertain whether or not the student is learning. The reality is that students **have control of what they learn**, and it greatly depends on their level of motivation.

The complex task of motivating each student should appear **before**, **during** and **after** the course. That is why it is necessary to use motivation techniques that will make the course content more relevant to the public.

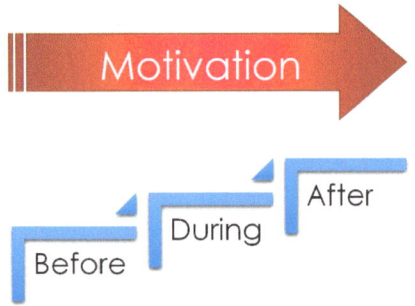

Figure 5-6: Motivation

There are multiple motivation techniques used throughout the training process for the achievement of the course by the students.

- **Establish a trust circle:** by initial interview, continuous tutoring, forums, chat, telephone inquiries ...
- **Confidence Environment:** attractive and friendly platform, interactive spaces and sound stimuli (melodies and songs).

A guidance to Blended Learning

- **Continuous Feedbacks:** recognition of work well done, positive and continuous support with phrases and words of encouragement.
- **Mentoring:** students act as experienced guides for the less experienced.
- **Collaborative learning:** through teamwork, wikis, blogs, learning communities.
- **Curiosity Stimulation.**
- **Scores:** this way the spirit of achievement will increase.

5.2.2. Technical Aspects

For some authors (Clarenc, 2013), the main function of a LMS is to manage and monitor student learning, participation and performance associated with all types of training[31].

However, in the development of this work, we see that all the functions of a LMS cover a much wider field, as it not only aims to create a virtual environment for learning but also it becomes a real experience.

This is achieved by integrating teaching materials and tools for communication, collaboration and educational management.

The main functions that must to be accomplished by LMS is to manage users, the resources, content and activities for teaching a particular subject; scheduling, organizing and managing events; manage access; control and monitor the learning process; have tools to assess; generate progress reports; manage communication services (such as discussion forums and video conferences, amongst others); enable collaboration between users and enable online conversation.

In short, one could say that a LMS serves to make the reflective methodology in the teaching organization available to students, as well as materials, tasks, forums, chat (amongst others) created by a group of teachers to promote learning in a particular area.

The basic features of an LMS should be:

- Interactivity
- Flexibility
- Scalability
- Standardization
- Usability
- Ubiquity
- Persuasability

---

[31] Clarenc, C. A.; S. M. Castro, C. López de Lenz, M. E. Moreno y N. B. Tosco (Diciembre, 2013). *Analizamos 19 plataformas de e-Learning: Investigación colaborativa sobre LMS*. Grupo GEIPITE, Congreso Virtual Mundial de e-Learning. Sitio web: www.congresoelearning.org

In line with the 7 minimum requirements that LMS should have, as discussed above, of which the environment is considered as appropriate - or optimal - it is necessary to allow the widest possible implementation of the following features:

Administrative Management	Resource Management	Communication Tools
Student Management/Monitoring Tools	Authorial and Editing Control	Forum
Mechanism Database Access	Learning Objects and other Content Management	Chat
Reporting	Templates for helping in creating content	Blackboard
Qualitative and Functional Management Workflow	Mechanisms for upstreaming and down streaming contents	E-mail
User Tracking	Re-use and Sharing Learning Objects	Wiki

Table 5-1: Minimum requirements for LMS

In this theme an analysis of the learning tools by Josep .M. Boneu (2007) is found, which is very useful and interesting and is summarized in the following table:

Tools	Description
Learning oriented	Forums, search forums, support for multiple formats, e-portfolios, file sharing, synchronous communication (chat), asynchronous communication (messaging, e-mail), blogs (weblog groups, individual and subject's blogs), multimedia presentations (videoconferencing), and wikis.
Productivity oriented	Personal notes or bookmarks, calendars and progress reviews, course finders, help with using the platform, synchronization mechanisms and work offline publishing control, expired pages and links, and course news.
Student involvement	Working groups, self-assessments, study groups, student profiles.
Support	User authentication, student registration and auditing.
Course and content publication	Tests and automated test results, administration course, student tracking, support from the course creator, rating online.
Curricular Design	Accessibility compliance, re-use and sharing of contents, templates courses environment customization (looking and feeling), according to the design of education (IMS – Instant Messaging System, AICC – Aviation Industry CBT[Computer-Based Training] Committee and ADL- Advanced Distributed Learning)

Figure 5-7: Analyses of the learning tools (Boneu 2007)

Although we are not going to make a comparative analysis of learning platforms, we will mention the most commonly used ones, in three categories: Open Source LMS, Commercial LMS and Cloud LMS. A comparative analysis can be seen in "Plataformas abiertas de e-learning para el soporte de contenidos educativos abiertos" (Boneu 2007).

Open Source LMS: ATutor, Chamilo, Claroline, Dokeos, .LRN, Moodle, Sakai.

Commercial LMS: Almagesto, Blackboard, Edu 2.0, E-ducativa, FirstClass, Nixty, Saba, WizIQ.

Cloud LMS: Ecaths, Edmodo, Schoology, Udemy.

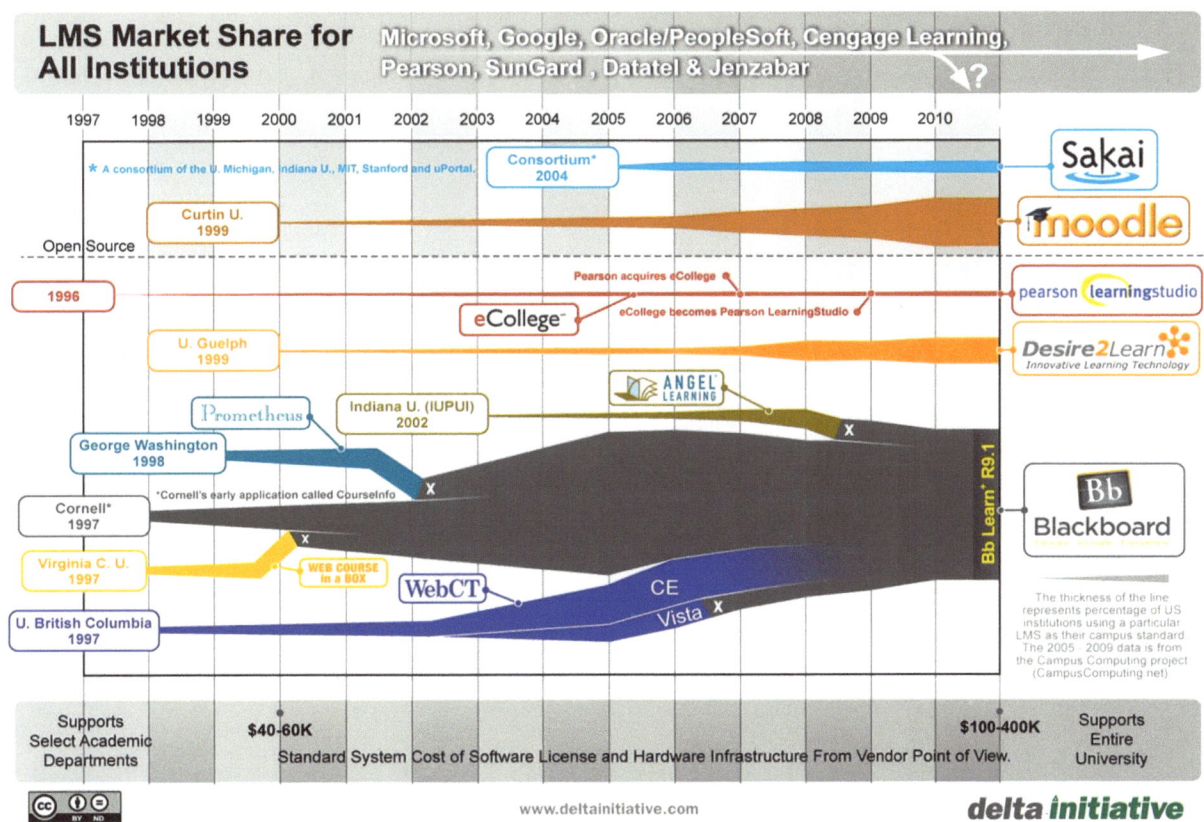

Figure 5-8: LMS Evolution (1997-2010) delta Initiative

Therefore, SAFA chose Moodle as its E-Learning platform following the above study. The virtual learning environment used in the SAFA Institution, as mentioned above, is Moodle. Throughout its existence it has evolved since the first version 1.5.4+ until version Moodle 2.5.4+ (Build: 20.140.228). There are two platforms, the students' platform and the teachers' platform.

Access to the Students' platforms done in two ways:
- For teachers (with fundacionsafa.es domain) and students (with safanet.es domain), both of them are made through "Brocal SAFA" (http://www.fundacionsafa.es) using OAuth2 protocol to access Google APIs as an authentication model.
- For students with e-mail accounts from any other domain, are made based on E-mail and direct access from http://www.safavirtual.com that has its own authentication ID.

Mainly, Google OAuth2 is used to gain access to the teacher's class, as this area is restricted to domains of SAFA Foundation. They are not allowed to use other access domains.

Infrastructure is supported by one Dell PowerEdge R410 server, where the platforms are stored with the following numbers of courses and users:

- Student platform (http://www.safavirtual.com): 974 courses and 11,196 users.
- Teacher platform (http://profes.safavirtual.com): 177 courses and 1,659 users.

5.3. Students' Expectation of an e-learning Platform

5.3.1. Trainees' needs

According to a research implemented by EDRASE and its partners (Tzimopoulos et al. 2013), trainees (primary and secondary education teachers) of an e-learning course, experienced the use of a Moodle platform very handy (mean value of satisfaction: 3,9/5). The main problems they encountered are presented in Table 5-2:

Kind of problem reported	Percentage of the answers %
Use of the Moodle platform	14,29
Tools provided by the trainers	2,52
Difficulties for completing the assignments.	10,09
Internet connection problems, especially in small islands	10,09
Incomprehensible assignment instructions.	5,04
Communication problems with other trainees.	7,56
Lack of time for completion of activities	13,44
No problem.	36,97

Table 5-2: The main problems encountered by trainees.

The general remarks made by the trainers combined, are presented in Table 5-3:

	Percentage of the answers %
The course was lengthy	5,48
Desire for more communication with trainees and trainers	15,07
Gained satisfaction from the course.	79,45
Total	100

Table 5-3: General remarks of the trainers concerning a blended learning course

Other issues of satisfaction for the trainees were:

- The course content was very satisfactory and useful for their job (teaching).
- The trainers took advantage of the knowledge attained and used it for personal improvements.
- There was an increase of the trainees' self-esteem in using ICT.

Some remarks of dissatisfaction were:

- The learning load was too heavy.
- The learning load was too light.
- The course content was not applicable for use in the teaching procedure.

Not only issues of the trainees are of interest also the problems realized by the trainers are an important part of evaluation. The different trainers' opinions are evaluated and presented in the following table:

General evaluation	Experience gain	Platform usage level of difficulty	Educational material	Activities	Major means of communication		
4.4/5	4.8/5	3.9/5	4.4/5	4.4/5	e-mail,	ooVoo	Moddle platform

Table 5-4: Trainers' opinion. (Adapted: Nikolaos Tzimopoulos, 2013)

The following three lists display main problems during the course encountered by the trainers. The main negative and positive aspects they experience during the course are listed as well. The positive comments are mainly approving the usage of online tools in order to create a good learning atmosphere.

Main problems of the trainers:

- Lack of time to deal with the course efficiently
- Technical difficulties using the platform

Positive aspects:

- Clarity in the announcement of activities
- Structure and material of the seminar
- Teachers' education in remote islands
- Usage of up to date web 2.0 tools
- Creation of large internet groups and a learning society
- Feeling of "belonging to a learning community"

Main negative aspects:

- Platform delay
- Problems with specific assignments
- Tough environment

Due to the fact that learners' needs are also connected to the possibilities offered by the institution as well as the subject matter the following table provides a review trainee's needs by various scientists.

Learners' needs	Reference
Interested in topic	Sonja Gabriel (2014)
Should not be forced	Sonja Gabriel (2014)
Basic IT skills	Sonja Gabriel (2014)
Requirements should be announced before	Sonja Gabriel (2014)
Not much availability of time to be present at the classroom	Patricia Aresta Branco (2014)
Being physically far from the place where the training is given	Patricia Aresta Branco (2014)
The trainee must be highly motivated to achieve training objectives and be very proactive	Branco Patricia Aresta (2014)
The student should be continually informed on every detail, in order to do proper planning and be well adjusted to the course schedule	Branco Patricia Aresta (2014)
The student must enter daily the computer platform, check for updates, get to know her/his tasks and plan them in time	Branco Patricia Aresta (2014)
The student must comply with the deadlines for the delivery of work and the activities in the platform; to have good results and not to accumulate work, which might cause anxiety and stress.	Branco Patricia Aresta (2014)
There should be monitoring of the questions raised and the work developed by the students.	Branco Patricia Aresta (2014)
On-line support is essential, and should be constant and permanent.	Branco Patricia Aresta (2014)
The quality of the manuals, the bibliography and the proper maintenance of the learning platform are of utmost importance	Branco Patricia Aresta (2014)

Table 5-5: Review of Learners' needs

5.3.2. Project evaluation on trainees' needs.

A) Method

During October and November 2014, the consortium partners distributed an online questionnaire on learners' needs. The questionnaire was mainly sent to students of previous and current e-learning courses. The answers of 1004 individuals were collected. Of course, not everybody replied all the questions asked. The origins of the learners were allocated over Europe as shown in the table below.

Albania	Austria	Finland	Fyrom	Greece	Italy	Romania	Spain	Turkey
1	34	24	4	571	152	4	211	3

Table 5-6: Overview of the origins of all learners.

All the different replies, some of them in mother tongue, were translated and combined in order to analyse all the results.

B) Questionnaire

In the following paragraph, the questions of the online survey are listed. The Learners had to fill in the online questionnaire with 15 closed and one open question.

1. How important do you consider is having clear instructions about how to get started and how to find various course components on the platform?
2. How important is the ease of use of the platform and support service (manuals, tutorials, help desk)?
3. How important is for the platform to cover both the face-to-face training activities and the virtual ones?
4. How important is to have a personalized entry page when logging-into the platform (i.e., showing my progress, which chapters I have to revise, etc.)?
5. Is it important that most learning activities are concentrated inside the platform instead of being distributed among many different tools available on the Internet?
6. How important are collaborative working tools within the platform?
7. How important are one-to-one private messaging tools between students and/or students and tutors within the platform?
8. How important is that the platform incorporates gamification elements and/or game mechanisms (rewards, scores, votes, ...)?
9. How important is for the platform to be connected to external social media (Facebook, LinkedIn, Pinterest, YouTube, google+, ...)?
10. How important is that the platform can manage groups of learners with the possibility of differentiating resources and activities among separate groups?
11. How important is for the learner to be allowed to customize the platform to better suit his/her needs?
12. How important is to find materials and information on the platform easily?
13. How important is a genuinely interactive way of studying on the platform?
14. How important is for working methods and activities on the platform to be new to the learner, so to try new ways of studying?
15. How important is the level of interaction with teachers and tutors through the platform?
16. Are there any other issues about the platform in a blended course that you want to suggest?

In the first 15 closed questions, the learners had to choose a value between 1 and 4 in order to evaluate the importance of certain platform properties. In this questionnaire the different values stand for

1 = Meaningless, 2 = Less important, 3 = Important and 4 = Very important. In the 16th question, learners had to write their own opinion regarding e-learning platforms.

C) Results

The great majority of the people rated the asked questions as *important* or *very important*. The following results will describe the outcomes of the questionnaire (mean value of 3.88 and a standard deviation of 0.49).

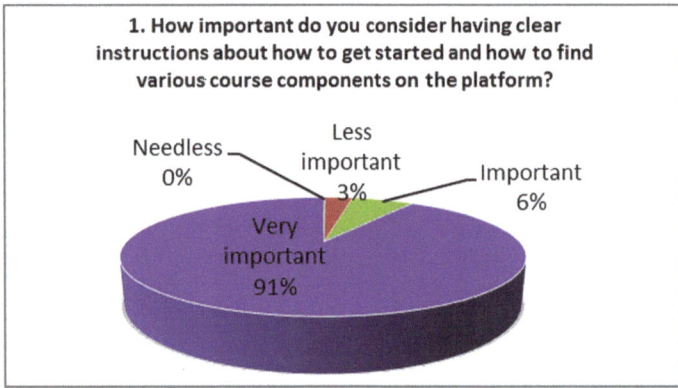

Figure 5-9: Importance of clear instructions

The learners want to have clear instructions about how to get started and how to find various course components on the platform (Figure 5-9). This fact could also be validated in the blended course held at the Vienna University of Technology. The learners need an introduction in new tools.

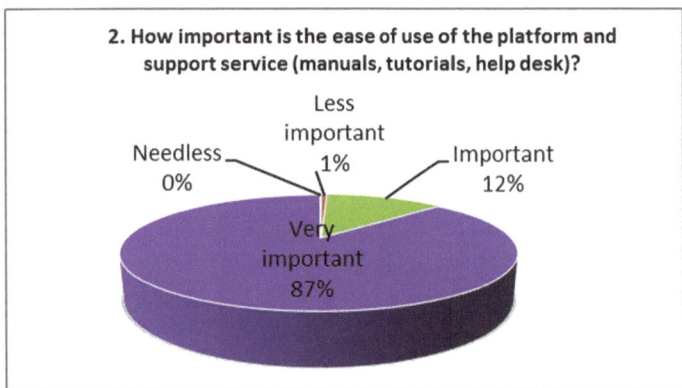

Figure 5-10: Ease of use of the platform and support

Additional to a certain instruction an easy handling of the platform and the support services (Figure 5-10) is necessary in order to motivate the learners to practice not only using books but also include the online environment (mean value of 3.86 and a standard deviation of 0.37).

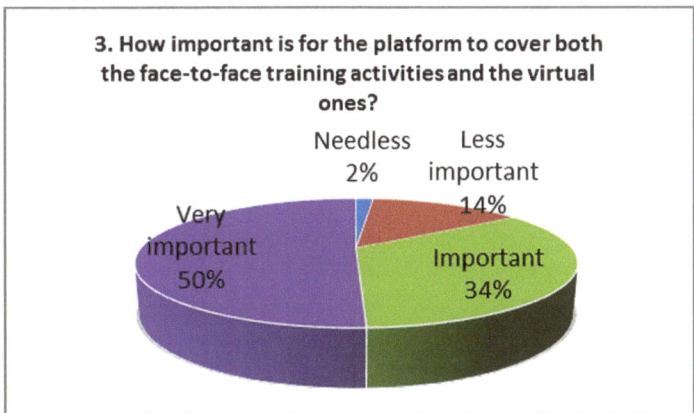

Figure 5-11: face-to-face and virtual activities covered by the platform

Compared to the first two questions the answers suggest that only half of the people think that the platform has to cover both face-to-face training activities and virtual ones (mean value of 3.34 and standard deviation of 0.83). This might be a matter of generation. A face-to-face meeting up to now did not require any online tools.

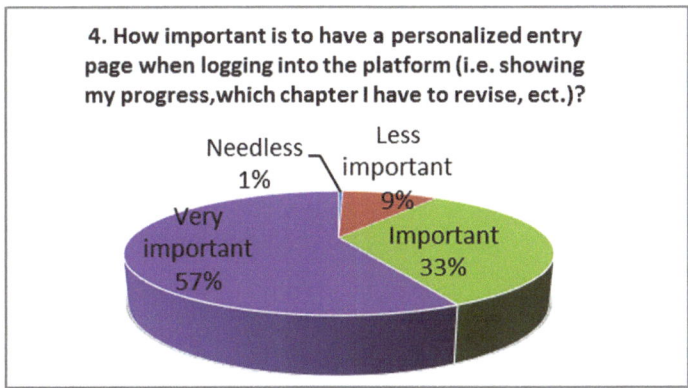

Figure 5-12: Importance of personalization

A more important issue is a personalized entry page after logging in the platform (Figure 5-12, mean value of 3.47 and standard deviation of 0.68). Nowadays everything seemed to be personalized to generate a trust between user and environment. Especially for learners this process is very important. In some cases the personalization also includes individual learning packages due to certain knowledge tests or homework (Landenfeld 2014, p.201-214).

Figure 5-13 shows the importance of the inclusion of most learning activities in the platform instead of being distributed among many different tools available on the Internet. This might be not very surprising because a confusing system can lead to demotivation. This also can be connected to the first questions. If the instruction and explanation of different tools is done properly some different tools supporting different learning phases could be used. Due to the fact that new versions of well-known platforms often offer new features it makes additionally tools redundant (mean value of 3.59 and standard deviation of 0.76).

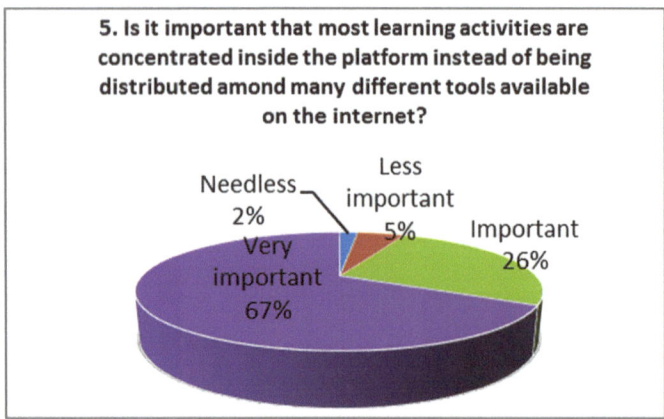

Figure 5-13: Importance of only ONE platform including most of the activities

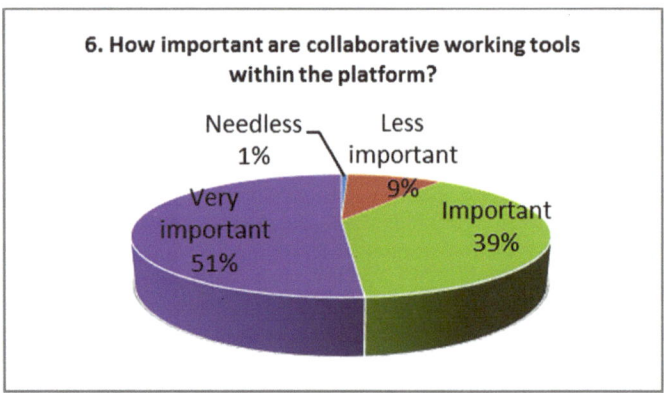

Figure 5-14: Answers of the sixth question with a mean.

The availability of collaborative working tools within the platform (Figure **5-14**, value of 3.41 and standard deviation of 0.73 were used) is also important. It is proven that right group building improves the learning progress (Kilpatrick 1999, p 129-144)

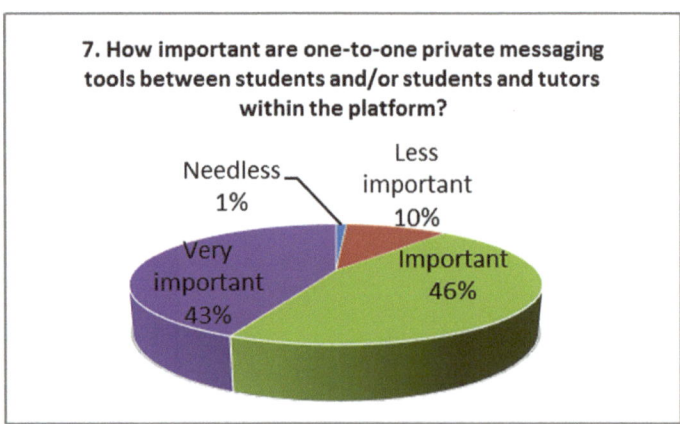

Figure 5-15: The importance of one-to-one messaging tools between students.

A guidance to Blended Learning

The learners expressed their preference of one-to-one private messaging tools among students as well as students and tutors within the platform (Figure 5-15, mean value of the seventh question is 3.31 with a standard deviation of 0.68). The need of this feature is not so urgent. It is an important but not the most important tool, which should be provided. A reason might be the availability using email or even other social communication tools. Therefore, some of the project members are already trying to include social media in their courses to be more attractive for the learners.

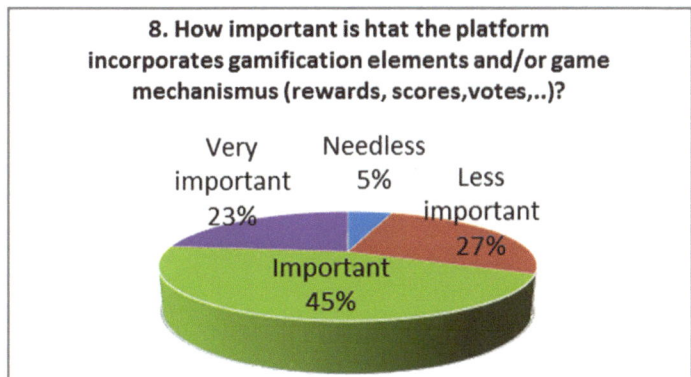

Figure 5-16: The importance of gamification inside the platform.

The platform should also incorporate gamification elements or game mechanisms (Figure 5-16, mean value of the eighth question is 2.87 with a standard deviation of 0.85). Compared to the questions before one can see that the relevance of gaming is not that important. One explanation could be the average age of the sample. At least 30% voted this issue as non-essential.

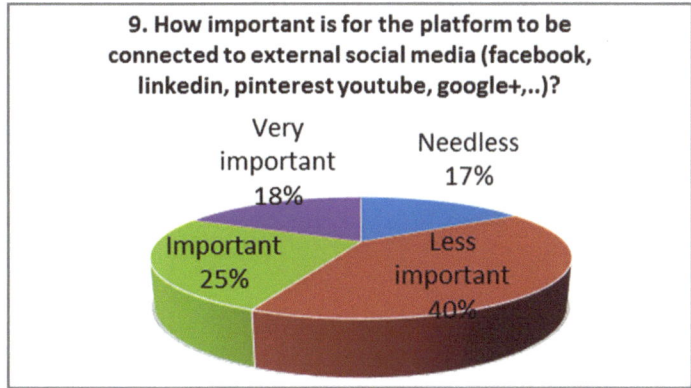

Figure 5-17: Importance of an existing connection to external social media.

Not many participants believed that it is important to have the platform connected to external social media (Figure 5-17, mean value 2.45 with a standard deviation of 1.02). More than 50% decided that social media should not or at least don't have to be linked. Perhaps some of them want to differ between learning, work and leisure time. If they are using social media they might want to keep it separate. But more than 40% could imagine a connection.

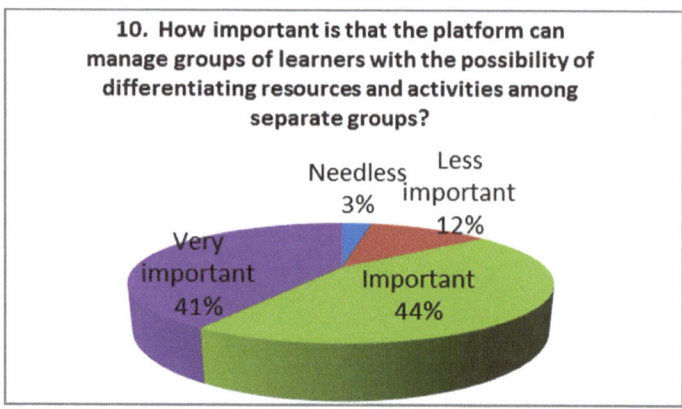

Figure 5-18: *Importance of group management of the platform*

They preferred the platform to manage groups of learners with the possibility of differentiating resources and activities among separate groups (Figure 5-18, mean value 3.24 and standard deviation 0.74).

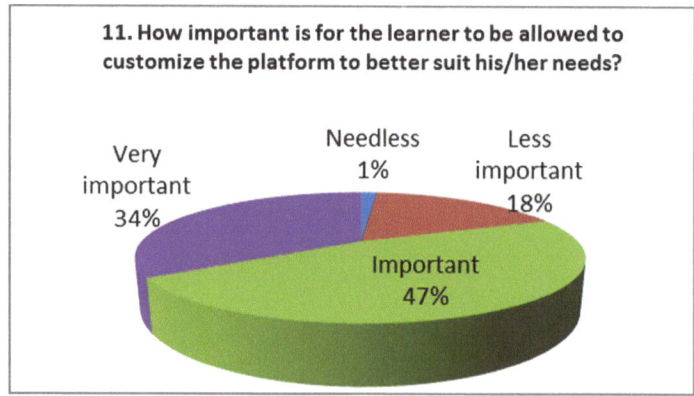

Figure 5-19: *Learners can customize the platform to adapt it better to their needs.*

The learners want to have influence on the appearance of the platform (Figure 5-19, mean value of the eleventh question with 990 answers is 3.14 with a standard deviation of 0.73). An appropriate customization helps the learners to have a better and more important modifiable overview materials and tasks.

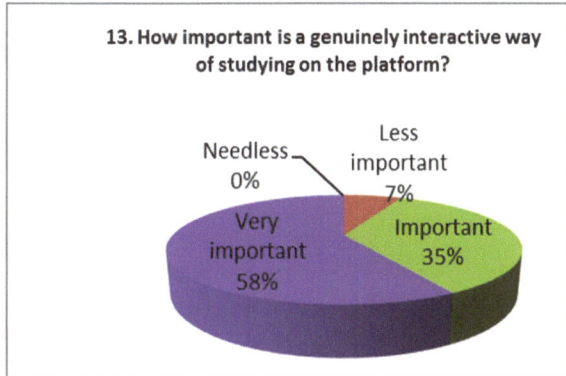

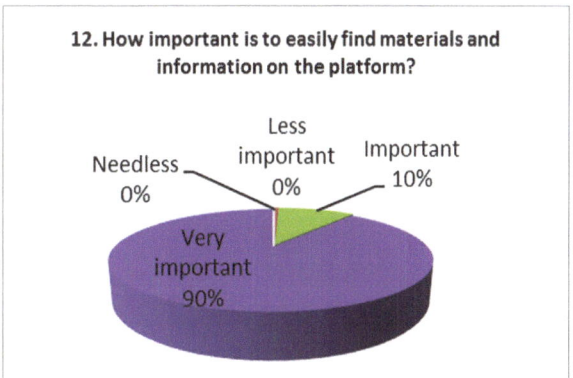

Figure 5-20: *Importance of an interactive way*

Figure 5-21: *Importance to find material easily*

They expressed their importance of finding materials and information easily (Figure 5-21). This should be a basic requirement of a platform. Due to the fact that not everything is as simple as it seems an appropriate evaluation of the platform in advance is for sure necessary. It is also quite important to have the possibility of a genuinely interactive way of studying on the platform (Figure 5-20).

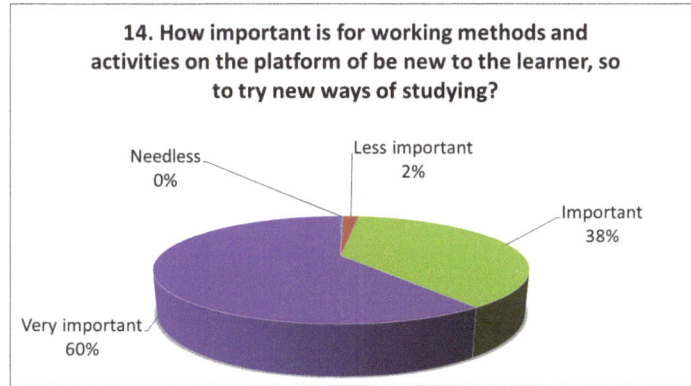

Figure 5-22: *Importance of innovations at the platform.*

The learners believe that innovative working methods and activities on the platform as well as their level of interaction with their tutors (figure 5-22, mean value of the 14th question with 902 answers is 3.44 with a standard deviation of 0.75.) increase their motivation during the learning process.

The level of interaction was also important for most the trainees (Figure 5-23, mean value of the 15th question with 993 answers is 3.46 with a standard deviation of 0.66).

15. How important is the level of interaction with teachers and tutors through the platform?

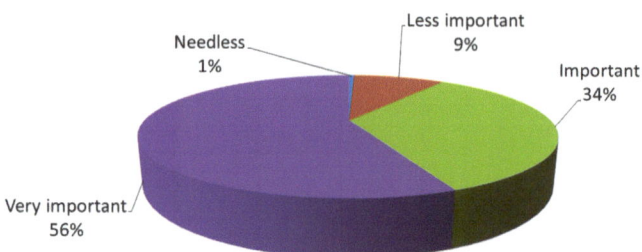

Figure 5-23: The importance of interaction with their tutors

Totally, 107 trainees sent their suggestions proposed in question 16. These suggestions were categorized in the following 8 themes:

- requesting for direct application to their needs
- encountered problems with the line connectivity
- Enquiry of more chances for interaction
- organizational issues encountered during the course
- platform connection issues
- tutorial support provided
- educational issues experienced in the course
- General suggestions

The goal of this research was to help the consortium members to design methodologies that might enable them to probe into different parts of the system and understand what is happening in the wider field of e-learning itself. Furthermore, they carefully analysed the responses to gain knowledge of the system parts. In this way, they obtained a better understanding of complex dynamic systems and the diversity inherent to such systems.

The results of this research will be used to define the quality criteria for a Blended Learning course, adopting Castells' view that (Castells 2001, p 28):

". . . we engage in a process of learning by producing, in a virtuous feedback between the diffusion of technology and its enhancement ... It is a proven lesson from the history of technology that users are key producers of the technology, by adapting it to their uses and values, and ultimately transforming the technology itself".

The survey was conducted to learners from 9 different countries who had attended different e-learning or blended learning courses with a majority of learners coming from Greece, Spain and Italy.

5.4. Quality Criteria for a Blended Learning Platform

5.4.1. Introduction

Our objective is to create a list of absolutely necessary features for the eLearning platform (LMS) used in a blended Learning course. These features are focused on the technical and pedagogical background as well as on the learner's situation. In addition, recommends for useful features and tools are defined that used either inside the LCMS or as additional tools.

The target of the blended learning platform is the provision of high quality learning that will lead to the development of the 21st century skills. These are characterized, according to Kong et al.(2014) by **three** emphases:

First emphasis is on skills development in both formal and informal learning contexts (Cox, 2013; Huang, Kinshuk. & Spector. 2013). The learners will be engaged in a seamless learning environment to coherently apply various generic skills for in-school teacher-led learning process initiated in digital classrooms and after-school learner-initiated learning process in social learning platforms/tools according to individual needs (Milrad, Wong, Sharpies, Hwang, Looi, & Ogata. 2013; Otero, Milrad, Rogers, Santos, Verissimo, & Tones. 2011; Wong & Looi. 2011).

Second emphasis is on skills development through both individualized and collaborative learning approaches. On their own or with peers, learners take responsibilities to apply various generic skills to plan goals, implement tasks, monitor progress and evaluate outcomes in their learning process (Kicken, Brand-Gruwel, Merrienboer, & Slot. 2009; Norris & Soloway. 2009). The feedback for learners in a minimal but sufficient amount identifies individual needs and directions for future improvement (Caballero, van Riesen, Alvarez, Nussbaum, De Jong. 2014; Sims. 2003: Van Merrienboer. & Sluijsmans. 2009).

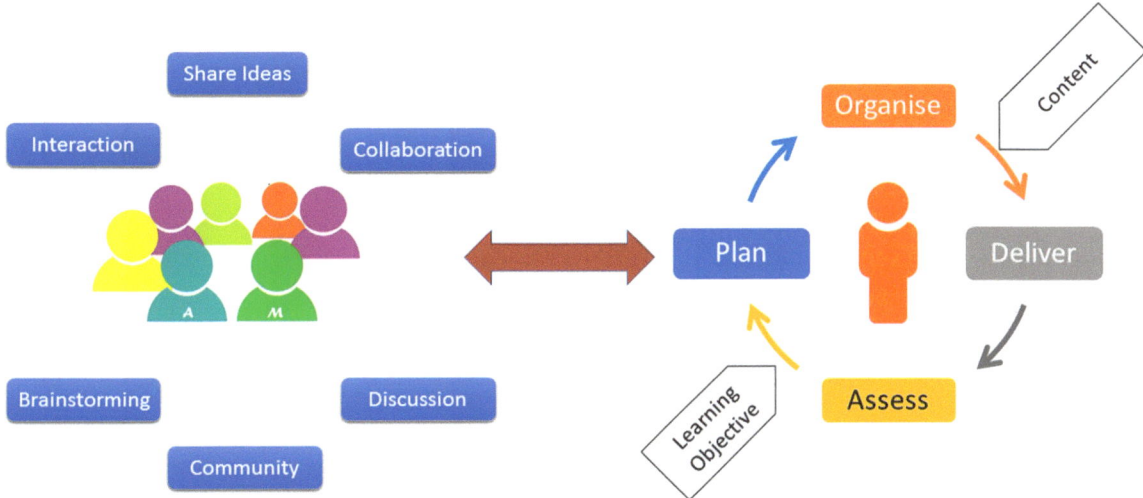

Figure 5-24: *Learning with Tech trends*[32]

---

[32] Adapted from Olenka Villavicencio (2013): Learning with Tech trends
(Retrieved from http://olevilla.blogspot.gr/2013_07_01_archive.html) and Planning for Personalization,(retrieved from http://education.vermont.gov/plp-working-group/main).

Third emphasis is on skills development supported by evidence of improvement and awareness of progress. The learning process in the e-leaning environment can be designed in a range of activities in authentic learning contexts. Rich evidence of improvement and productive failure is collected by learners' performance during the learning process; indications on applying 21st century skills for processing real-life information, reflecting on problem-solving ways, articulating tacit knowledge and negotiating multiple analysis perspectives for knowledge construction are provided (Herrington & Kervin. 2007; Niederhauser & Lindstrom. 2006; Zualkeman. 2006). Learners and teachers are given many opportunities of improvement and reflection on progress in the e-leaning environment, due to a continuous formative assessment throughout the learning process and the summative assessment in particular stages.

Figure 5-25: The course improvement process[33]

5.4.2. Definitions

According to the "Guide for designing and developing e-learning courses" (FAO, 2011), "…a learning platform is a set of interactive online services that provide learners with access to information, tools and resources to support educational delivery and management through the Internet".

Usually, there are 3 kinds of learning platforms:

- Virtual learning environments (VLEs),
- Llearning management systems (LMSs) or
- Learning content management systems (LCMSs).

These definitions have no clear limits and are often used interchangeably. There are certainly differences among them but some of the features of these platforms are common.

---

[33] Retrieved from **PPLG's Assessment Literacy & Development®** (http://www.p2learninggroup.com/assessment.html)

Virtual learning environments (VLE). These are learning platforms used to simulate traditional face-to-face classroom activities and facilitate teaching and learning. Their main characteristic is their strong collaborative component. The most well-known VLEs are "Moodle" and "Blackboard".

Learning Management System (LMS). Using this kind of learning platforms, we can facilitate the delivery and management of all learning offerings, including online, virtual classroom and instructor-led courses. It also automates the learning course, delivers the training easily, manages learners and keeps track of their progress and performance across training activities, and, therefore, reduces administrative load (FAO, 2011).

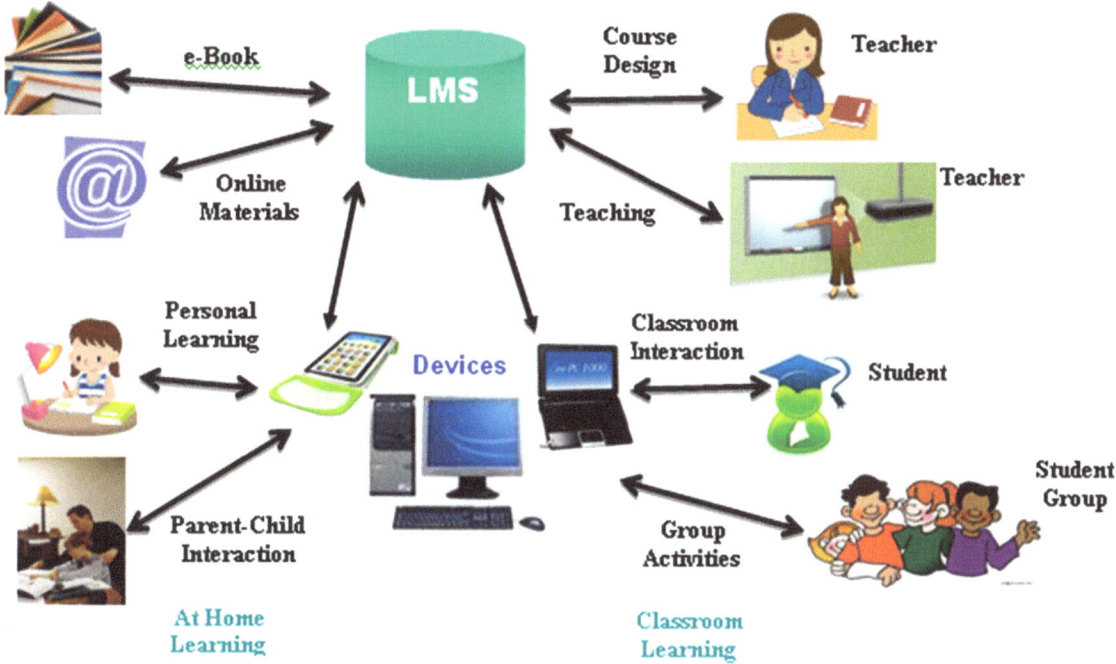

Figure 5-26: LMS dependencies in Blended Learning (Source: Gaul 2014)

The differences between VLE and LMS come more from the setting in which they operate. LMSs are primarily appointed to training while VLEs focuses on education. The well-known Moodle platform is considered to be an LMS, but it is also referred as a VLE in the education sector, promoting a communicative and collaborative approach.

An LMS is used by training administrators to manage all aspects of learning and development, such as skill/competency, personal development plans, learning content management, reporting and workflow.

VLE, instead, supports facilitated online learning within education institutions and allows tutors and students to share content. This means that VLEs do not necessary contain all the content within them – they may only provide links to certain content pages. VLEs are increasingly being adopted as LMS replacements; products like Moodle or Blackboard originally adopted for the education institutions are now widely used by the corporate market for online and blended solutions delivery.

The 3rd type of learning platform, the "**learning content management system**" (LCMS) – focuses mainly on creating an e-learning content. Therefore, it is used mainly by developers and administrators to create content material for e-learning and blended learning courses. This material includes articles, tests, games,

video and small units of digital content, called content chunks. In this way, these components can easily been assembled and reused into different courses according to learners' needs. LCMSs reduce development efforts and allow digital content to be easily repurposed.

5.4.3. Proposed Quality criteria

A) Technical Issues: A learning platform should:
- Have a user friendly design
- Be working even with low internet speed connection.
- Have many communication tools.
- Have many collaborative tools (for example wiki, Google docs).
- Be customized, according to the trainees' needs.
- Be stabilized, not presenting any technical problems.
- Have continuous updating and compatibility with previous versions.
- Be provided with a continuous technical problem solving forum.
- Have the possibility of splitting the trainees into virtual classes.
- To be available in many languages.

B) Aesthetic issues: A learning platform should:
- Have a welcoming atmosphere with attractive pictures and friendly greeting texts so as to motivate and guide trainees conduct toward style.
- Have an introducing pace that indicates important milestones or tasks.
- Provide trainees with high demands on transparency of information regarding the course organization and the course schedule.
- Have structure, which allows a rapid orientation to all participants and corresponds to the concept of the offer. This structure should not be too complex, e.g. the list of folders should not get longer or a nested system should have subfolders.

C) Pedagogical issues: A learning platform should:
- Have interactive educational material.
- Have many small activities on a weekly basis to check the trainees' progress.
- Have activities given in a clear way and enhance active participation.
- Have weekly deliverables.
- Have teamwork activities, where ever necessary.
- Have the trainees informed about their progress in due course.
- Provide justified feedback, in a short time.
- Provide educational material that satisfies the trainees' real needs.
- Have a structure depended on contemporary teaching methods like team work, questions/answers, discussions, brain storming, role play, cases studies.

- Have a structure that gives trainees the feeling that they belong to a virtual classroom and are not isolated.
- Have a structure which helps the formation of trainees' sub-networks.

5.5. Tutorial Support for the Online Teaching

The idea of a perfect blended learning course itself is not enough to guarantee a success course. The organization and team behind the course influences the quality of the outcome significant. Due to the fact that blended learning courses include face-to-face meetings and online training there are two main aspects. The tutors and lectures have to attend a certain training course or at least a workshop in order to pursue the same goal not only in their personal opinion but also regarding the appearance for the learners. Nothing derogates a course more than a negative minded person on the team. The atmosphere of the team should be approving the blended learning structure. Learners are motivated if they can feel the passion of tutors and lecturers. One the other hand a good administrated eLearning system is important as well. If the lecturer is very dedicated but the organization and administration of the course materials and exercises is not done properly the blended learning course won´t succeed. The quality criteria for an appropriate eLearning platform were already discussed in the sections before. Therefore, this paragraph deals with the requirements within tutorial support.

5.5.1. What students expect from the course tutorial support

Tutorial support is an important part of a blending learning course. Therefore a survey was spread out using contacts of the consortium members as well as newsletters and postings. In December 2015 an online questionnaire was created. The questionnaire was mainly sent to students of previous and current e-learning courses. There were 267 responses from over 10 countries. The origins of most of the learners were in Europe. A detailed distribution is shown in Table 5-7.

Argentina	Austria	Czech Rep.	Germany	Greece	Italy	Romania	Serbia	Switzer-land	Ukraine
1	102	1	10	57	71	7	6	2	2

Table 5-7: Overview of the origins of learners' participation a survey about tutorial support.

A) Questionnaire

This section describes the structure of the questionnaire. First of all there were some questions regarding sex, age and origin of the learners in order to set the answers in a certain connection to age or sex. This was followed by 14 closed questions which had different answer proposals. Some of them where equally rated as in the survey regarding eLearning platforms using a four point system from meaningless to very important. Other questions ask for particular answers where the learners have to choose one of the proposed answers.

Communication
1. How important is a direct contact to the instructor of the course in meaning of a hotline?

2. How important are standards for instructor responses (return time for emails, etc.) and availability (office hours, etc.)?
3. How important are instructional activities for achieving learning objectives in the course or a certain module?
4. Which communication tool would you prefer to contact tutors or instructors? (Telephone, Skype, Chat or Forum)

Assignments/Homework
1. How important are time structured assignments which are only available at a certain time according to the course content?
2. How important is a regular summary of the taken lectures and exercises?
3. How important is a regular feedback of the instructors regarding your progress in the course (e.g. if you are behind the proposed schedule)?
4. How much time do you think an assignment should be available? (1 week, 2 or 3 weeks or even unlimited)

Self-Learning
1. Is it important to have education material in an interactive form?
2. How important is it to have educational goals stated?
3. Is it important to have educational materials in a multimedia form?
4. How important is the possibility of a self-evaluation of your own progress?
5. How important is a visualization of your progress inside the course, e.g. a bar showing the done work in proportion to all available exercises?
6. How important are effort comparison of all participants in an anonymous way?

Except of two questions had to choose a value between 1 and 4 which stands for
1 = Meaningless, 2 = Less important, 3 = Important and 4 = Very important.

B) Results

One of the questions was the sex of the learners. There were slightly more male persons answering the survey. In other words, 45% women and 55% men were asked. The distribution over age is more complex.

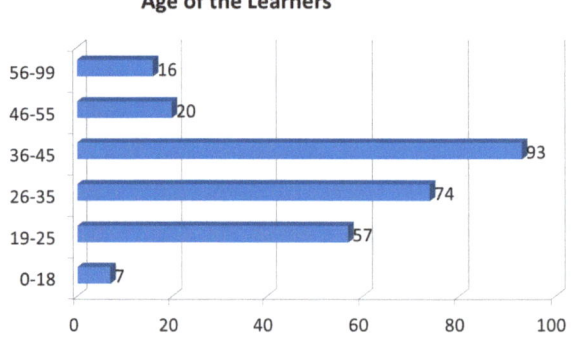

Figure 5-27: The number different ranges of age and number of questioners

Most of the answers were given by people between 19 and 45 years. For adult education, this range might be a little bit too big but more than a half are learners in the age of 26 to 45 which would be the perfect interest group.

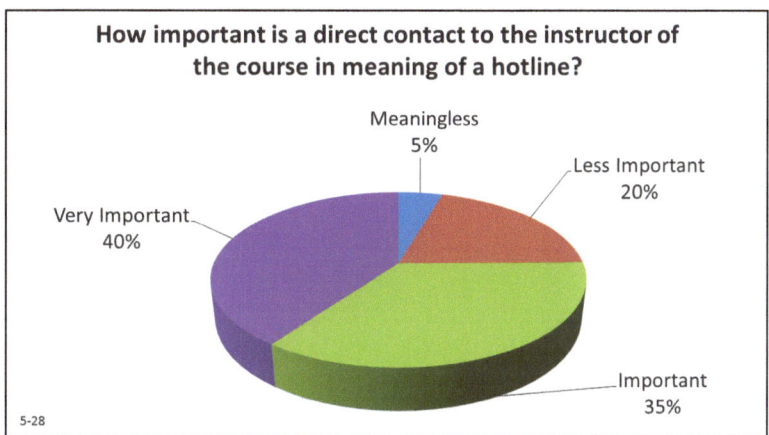

Figure 5-28: The importance of direct contact with the tutor.

Figure 5-28 shows that a direct hotline connecting to a tutor or lecturer is important (mean value of 3.11). A closer look on the data outlines a greater need regarding learners between 26 and 45 years old.

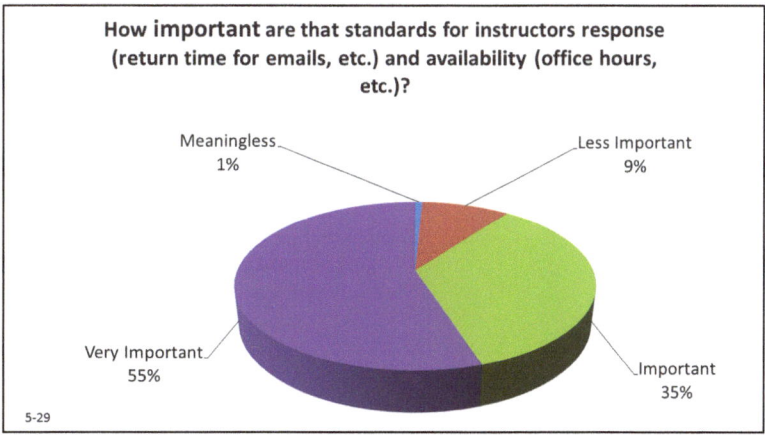

Figure 5-29: The importance of tutor contact.

The importance of certain standards regarding communication with instructors is very high (mean value of 3.44). The mean value is same through all age classes. There should be a defined schedule for availability but also a certain time span for responses which helps learners to coordinate their homework and duties in time.

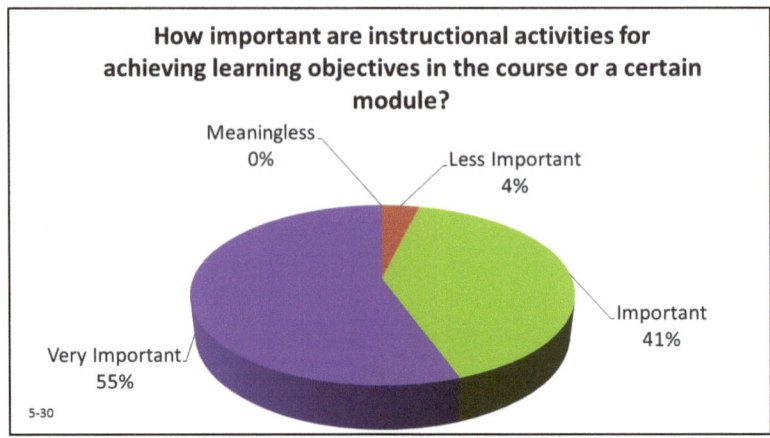

Figure 5-30: The importance of the instructional activities

The results of the third question suggest that a clear structure of the course is necessary (Mean value of the third question is 3.52). For every step or stage of the course there should be instructional activities leading to defined goals. An example for these goals could be on the one hand an ordinary homework but on the other hand, there could be an online task, e.g. a quiz including questions of the current stage. These quizzes could also be link in that way that a learner can only take the latest quiz if he or she has passed the old one. The small task spread over the course helps learners to stick to the topic.

Figure 5-31: The fourth question deals with different tools to contact instructors.

Obviously, the forum is the most common used communication tool. Direct contact to the instructor using telephone or Skype is not important. Also an active form of communication throughout a chat is also not required. An advantage of the forum might be that the questions and given answers are available at any time. It is not possible to look something up in an ordinary chat or a telephone call.

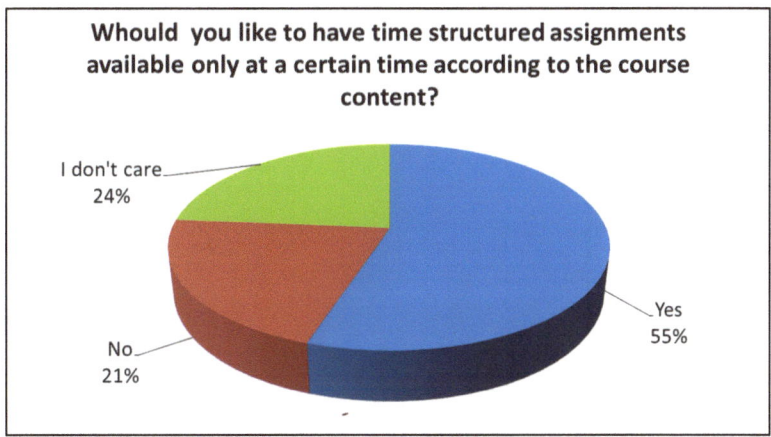

Figure 5-32: The fifth question asks about the availability of assignments.

Structured assignments can be different things. On the one hand it can mean that certain tasks are only available during a particular period of time. On the other hand it could also mean that the course materials are not available before the subject matter was not part of the course jet. Didactical speaking the first option would only be useful if the offered task should be done before the next part of the course starts to create a similar level of knowledge. The second option coordinates in some ways the learning process of the course participants. The relevant course materials are offered when the lecture or homework deals with this topic and not in advance. The only disadvantage might be that motivated learners will not have the possibility to read up on the next subject.

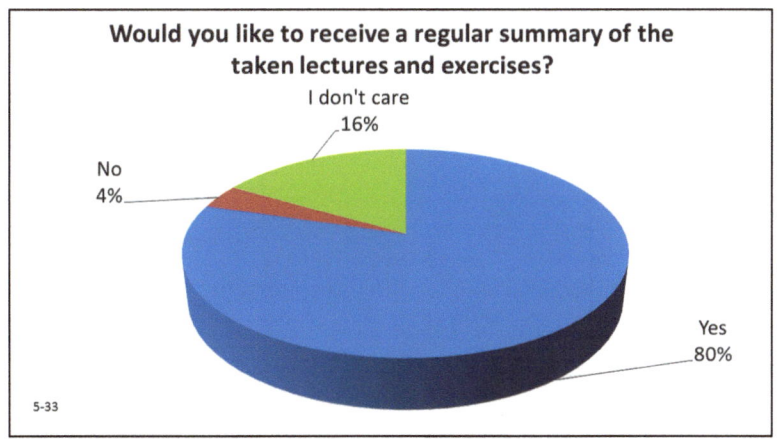

Figure 5-33: The sixth question asks if a regular summary is necessary

This question was answered quit clear. Most of the learners think that a regular summary of lectures and exercises is an important part of a blended learning course. This summary also enables learners to check if they have done all the exercises and know the main aspects of the last course part. This summary could also be important for the instructor to prepare the next part properly.

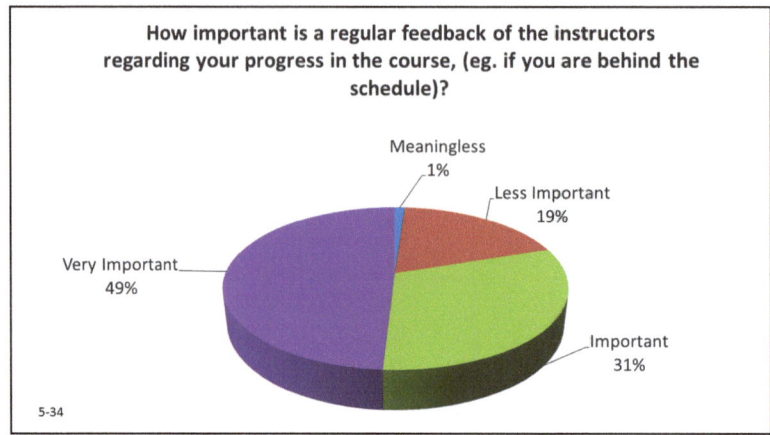

Figure 5-34: The seventh question deals with the course progress

Feedback regarding the course progress is important for 80% of the questioned learners (Figure 5-34). People thinking that it is not important, may be motivated enough to learn without visual reminder.

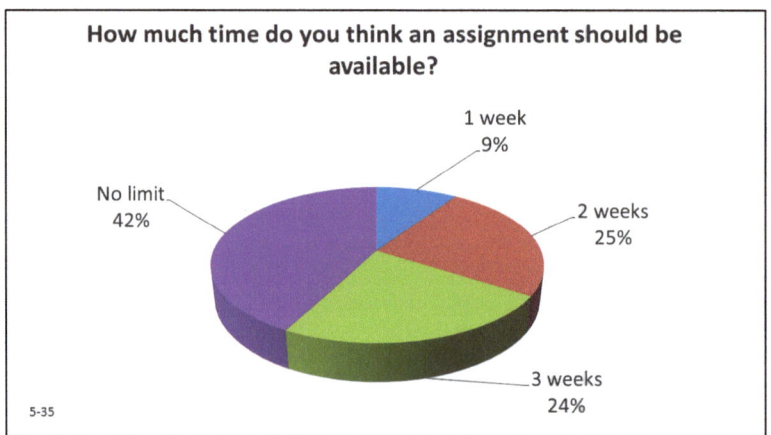

Figure 5-35: In the eighth question time restricted assignments are of interest.

Figure 5-35 shows that nearly a half of the learners want assignments available all the time. One quarter means that 3 weeks are enough the other quarter thinks that a restriction to 2 weeks is satisfying. The different age classes differ only a little bit. Learners between 36 and 45 agree more to restricted assignments than learners between 19 and 35 years. The new generation might be used to the fact that everything is available at any time due to internet nowadays.

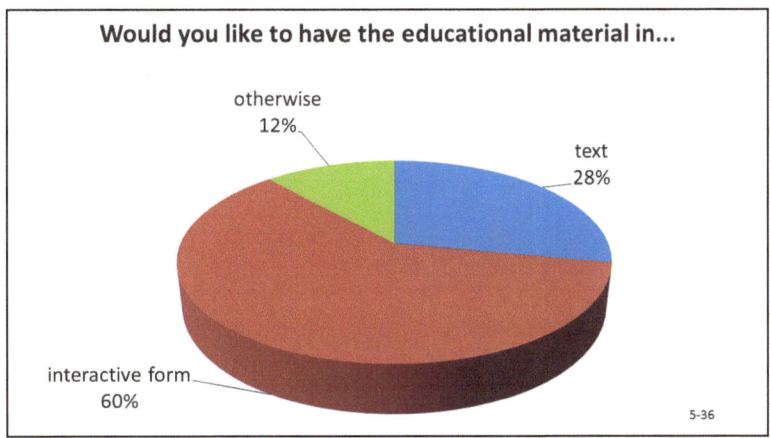

Figure 5-36: In the ninth question different educational materials are discussed.

In every class age the interactive education materials are most wanted (Figure 5-36). If someone is looking closer a stereotype can be found. The younger generations are more into interactive materials than the older ones. The interactive form can be seen as a playful learning method. Looking at different learners the opposite phenomena can be determined for picking text as favourite material.

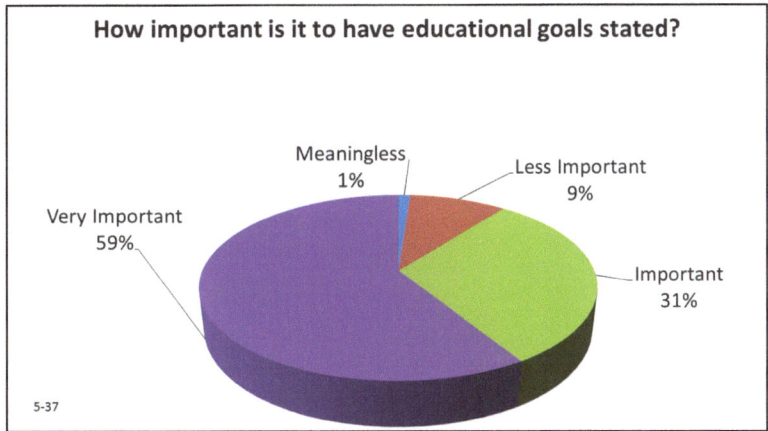

Figure 5-37: The tenth question asks about education goals.

Providing proper educational goals in a blended learning is very important to learners (Figure 32). Such goals clarify the aim and purpose of the course. It makes it easier to estimate the necessary effort in order to pass the course successfully.

A guidance to Blended Learning

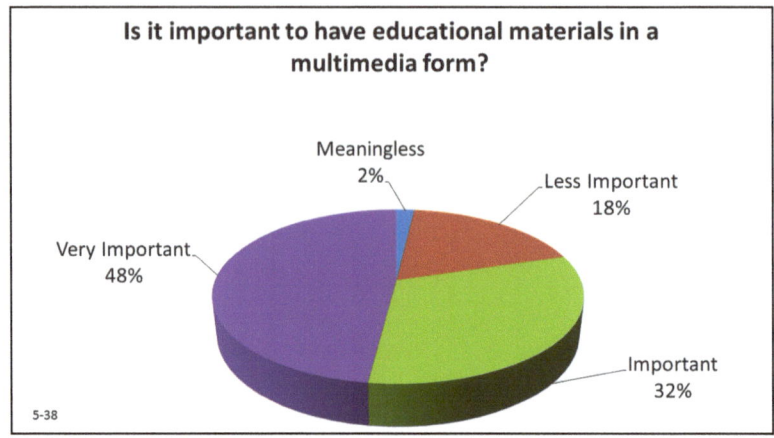

Figure 5-38: The eleventh question deals with multimedia materials for educational purpose.

It is also important to create educational materials using different forms. Not everything can be transformed in an interactive assignment. It should be a mixture of texts, videos or quizzes perhaps using an online platform. A fifths of the students would be satisfied with ordinary monotonously materials.

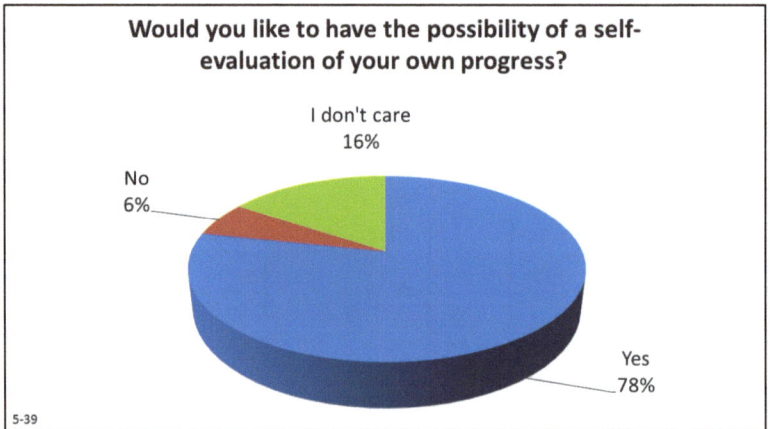

Figure 5-39: In the twelfth question, the learners decide if self-assessment is necessary.

Most of the learners appreciate small assignments which can be used to test their knowledge. Such small tests could help learners to check which parts of the course they should repeat and learn again.

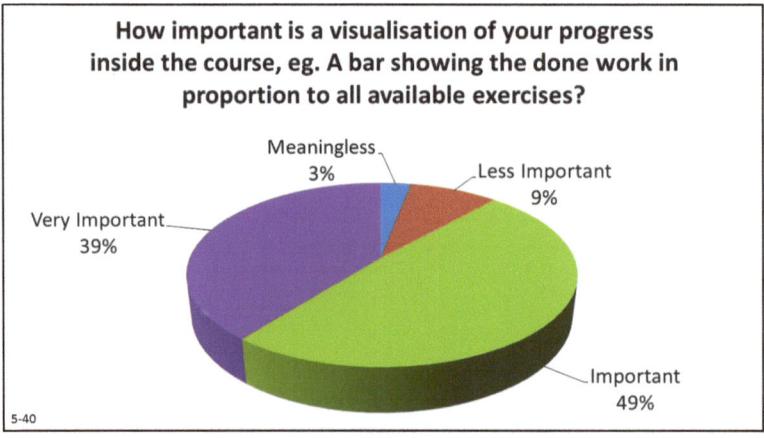

Figure 5-40: The thirteenth question asks if learners want a visualization of their progress.

A guidance to Blended Learning

The visualization of the learning progress is important for the learners (Figure 5-40). Compared to other questions before the mean value is only 3.25. If it is possible to provide such visualization in a course this might reminded learners to finish an assignment or a task whenever they look at the incomplete bar.

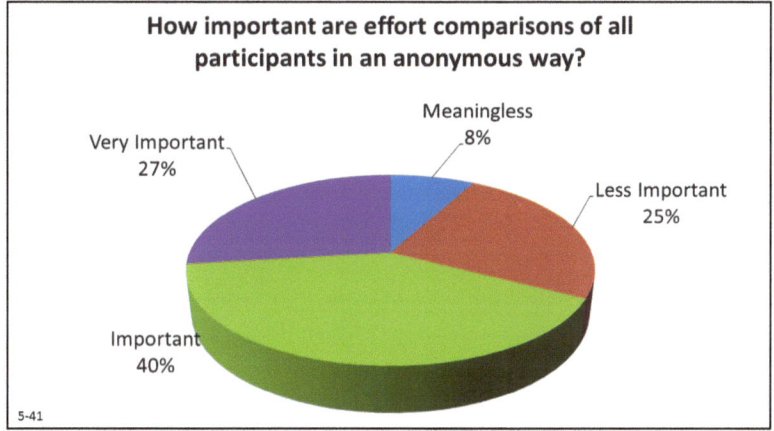

Figure 5-41: Replies about the importance of effort comparison

The low mean value suggests that a comparison with other participants is not necessary (The mean value of the last question is 2.87). On the one hand, it could lead to insecurity of some learners. On the other hand, it supports a maybe unwanted competition between the participants and makes it hard to work in groups or to help gaining team build competences.

5.5.2. Quality criteria to support students

The evaluation of the survey can be used to point out different important issues regarding tutorial support and support in order to improve the learning process. Due to former studies and research results as well as experiences of courses at the Vienna University of Technology additional aspects can be included in the list of criteria.

A) Technical Issues: Due to the fact that blended learning course require certain technical conditions in order to enable learners to participate in such courses.

- Lecture halls providing IT facilities in order to connect face-to-face and online phases
- Access to the online part of the course should be guaranteed for all students
- Availability of IT support for students (Email, Forum, etc.)
- Introduction in online environments for students

B) Pedagogical issues: There are different aspects, which should be minded by the instructors planning a blended learning course.

- Direct contact to the instructor in form of a forum with defined times of availability to guarantee immediate feedback or response in a certain time frame
- Offering educational materials in interactive and multimedia form
- Lectures are most effective using a combination of instructional strategies (discussion, group work, role-play, games, etc.)
- Preparation of materials and course structure in advance in order to formulate educational goals and learning objectives at the beginning of the course to equalize expectations of learner and instructor (sort of learning contract)
- Providing self-assessment tasks at the end of a course module

- Visualization of the learners progress in the course; can be combined with a regular feedback of the instructor
- Materials, tasks and assignments should be visible after dealing with the topic but then accessible until the end of the course
- Time-restricted assignments (2-3 weeks) might be useful for quizzes regarding certain course sections
- Regular summary of past lectures and exercises with additional links or possible materials for further reading and learning
- Surveys in order to adapt the course structure to changing conditions
- The instructors and tutors should have a workshop before starting the course requiring equal methods
- Before an exam the learners should be able to have a timeslot to ask question which arise during the learning phase; optional tutorials additional to the lecture to improve comprehension
- Offer an additional course regarding learning methods independent from subject matters

5.6. Sources

Alexander, S., Harper. C Anderson, T., Golja. T., Lowe. D., McLaughlan. R., Schaverien. L., & Thompson. D. (2006). Towards a mapping of the field of e-learning. In P. Kommers & G. Richards (Eds.). Proceedings of World Conference on Educational Multimedia, Hypermedia and Telecommunications 2006. Chesapeake. VA: AACE. 1636-1642. Retrieved November 27. 2006. from http: www.editlib.org mdex.cfm?ruseaction=Reader.ViewAbstract&paper_id=23224.

Boneu, J. (2007). *Plataformas abiertas de e-learning para el soporte de contenidos educativos abiertos.* Recuperado el octubre de 2012, de Revista de Universidad y Sociedad del Conocimiento RUSC: http://www.raco.cat/index.php/Rusc/article/viewFile/58133/68225

Bonk, C.J., & Graham, C.R. (2006). The handbook of blended learning environments: Global perspectives, local designs. San Francisco: Jossey-Bass/Pfeiffer. p.5

Branco, P. A. (2014), "Quality in Blended Learning"- NEEDS OF LEARNERS. Conference , Quality in Blended Learning" Wiener Neustadt, Austria 2014/20/02 - 2014/22 /05

Caballero, D., van Riesen, S., Alvarez, S., Nussbaum, M., & De Jong, T. (2014). The effects of whole-class interactive instruction with single display groupware for triangles. *Computers and Education*, *70*, 203-211.

Castells, M. (2001). The Internet Galaxy: Reflections on the Internet, Business, and Society, Oxford: Oxford, University Press.

Clarenc, C. A.; S. M. Castro, C. López de Lenz, M. E. Moreno y N. B. Tosco (Diciembre, 2013). *Analizamos 19 plataformas de e-Learning: Investigación colaborativa sobre LMS*. Grupo GEIPITE, Congreso Virtual Mundial de e-Learning. WWW: www.congresoelearning.org

Cox, M. J. (2013). Formal to informal learning with IT: Research challenges and issues for e-learning. *Journal of Computer Assisted Learning*, *29*(1), 85-105.

FAO (2011).E-learning methodologies. A guide for designing and developing e-learning courses. ISBN 978-92-5-107097-0

Friesen, Norm (2012). "Report: Defining Blended Learning", http://learningspaces.org/papers/Defining_Blended_Learning_NF.pdf

Gabriel, S. (2013) Personalizing Learning –Evaluation of an Austrian blended learning course. Paper presented in the conference about "Quality in Blended Learning" in Wiener Neustadt ,Austria, 20-23/2/2014.

Gaul, Cassandra (2014): GAVS – Discussing the LMS and the CMS | Kinetic ED on WordPress.com. Available online at https://kineticed.wordpress.com/2014/09/15/gavl-lms-v-cms/, checked on 9/4/2015.

Ginns, P., & Ellis, R. (2007). Quality in blended learning: Exploring the relations between on-line and face-to-face teaching and learning. Internet and Higher Education, 10, 53-64

Herrington, J., & Kervin, L. (2007). Authentic learning supported by technology: Ten suggestions and cases of integration in classrooms. *Educational Media International*, *44*(3), 219-236.

Hoić–Božić , **Nataša** (2008), A Blended Learning Approach to Course Design and Implementation.6th Workshop "Course Development in E-learning Environment". LOCATION: Rijeka, 25/09/2008.

Huang, R., Kinshuk, & Spector, J. M. (Eds.) (2013). *Frontiers of learning technology in a global context*. Berlin/Heidelberg, Germany: Springer.

Jackson & Schaverien (2005).Developing Research Designs and Methodologies for Investigating Learning in Post graduate e-Learning Contexts (2005)Paper presented at the AARE annual conference PARRAMATTA, 2005.

Kicken, W., Brand-Gruwel, S., Merriënboer, J., & Slot, W. (2009). Design and evaluation of a development portfolio: How to improve students' self-directed learning skills. *Instructional Science*, *37*(5), 453-473.

Kilpatrick S., Rowena B. & Falk I. (1999). The role of group learning in building social capital. In: Journal of Vocational Education & Training Vol51,Issue 1. p. 129-144. DOI: 10.1080/13636829900200074

Landenfeld K., Göbbels, M., Hintze A., Priebe J. (2014). viaMINT – Aufbau einer Online Lernumgebung für videobasierte interaktive MINT-Vorkurse. In: Zeitschrift für Hochschulentwicklung Jg. 9/Nr. 5 p.102-114. ISSN: 2219-6994.

Milrad, M., Wong, L. H., Sharples, M., Hwang, G.-J., Looi, C.-K., & Ogata, H. (2013). Seamless learning: An international perspective on next generation technology enhanced learning. In Z. L. Berge & L. Y. Muilenburg (Ed.), *Handbook of mobile learning* (pp. 95-108). New York, NY: Routledge.

Niederhauser, D. S., & Lindstrom, D. L. (2006). Addressing the nets for students through constructivist technology use in K-12 classrooms. *Journal of Educational Computing Research*, *34*(1), 91-128.

Norris, C., & Soloway, E. (2009). A disruption is coming: A primer on the mobile technology revolution. In A. Druin (Ed.), *Mobile technology for children: Designing for interaction and learning* (pp. 125-139). Amsterdam, The Netherlands: Elsevier Inc.

Otero, N., Milrad, M., Rogers, Y., Santos, A., Veríssimo, M., & Torres, N. (2011). Challenges in designing seamless learning scenarios: Affective and emotional effects on external representations. *International Journal of Mobile Learning and Organisation*, *5*(1), 15-27.

Ralston-Berg Penny (2014). Surveying Student Perspectives of Quality:Value of QM Rubric Items. Internet Learning Volume 3 Issue 1 - Spring 2014.

Sims, R. (2003). Interactivity and feedback as determinants of engagement and meaning in e-learning environments. In S. Naidu (Ed.), *Learning and teaching with technology: Principles and practices* (pp. 243-257). Sterling, VA: Kogan Page.

Tzimopoulos Nikolaos (2014). Blended Learning Seminar Evaluation from seminar trainers. Paper presented in the conference about "Quality in Blended Learning" in Wiener Neustadt ,Austria, 20-23/2/2014.

Van Merriënboer, J. J. G., & Sluijsmans, D. M. A. (2009). Toward a synthesis of cognitive load theory, four-component instructional design, and self-directed learning. Educational Psychology Review, 21(1), 55-66.

Wong, L. H., & Looi, C. K. (2011). What seams do we remove in mobile assisted seamless learning? A critical review of the literature. Computers and Education, 57(4), 2364-2381.

Zualkernan, I. A. (2006). A framework and a methodology for developing authentic constructivist e-Learning

Chapter 6:
The Assessment

Authored by: Felix Breitenecker
Andreas Körner
Stefanie Winkler
Language correction and final check:
Andreas Bauer

If you can´t measure it you can´t understand it.
If you can´t understand it, you can´t control it.
If you can´t control it, you can´t improve it.

H. James Harrington

Contents of Chapter 6

6. Assessment 95

    6.1. Assessments Classification 96

        6.1.1. Assessment types 96

        6.1.2. Methods and Question types 97

        6.1.3. Assessment Designs 97

        6.1.4. Feedback 98

    6.2. Assessment at TU Wien 99

        6.2.1. Refresher Course 99

        6.2.2. Basic and Advanced Mathematical Courses 99

        6.2.3. Simulation Courses 100

    6.3. Summary 100

        6.3.1. Quality of Assessment 100

        6.3.2. Choice of Assessment 101

    6.4. Sources 102

List of Figures

Figure 6-1: Usage of assessment in a Blended Learning course. 95

List of Tables

Table 6-1: Checklist for designing an assessment 101

6. Assessment

According to Boud (1995), all assessments including self-assessment comprise two main elements: making decisions about the standards of performance expected to enable judgements about the quality of the performance in relation to these standards. When self-assessment is introduced, it should ideally involve students in both of these aspects.

Andrade and Du. (2007, p.160) provide a useful definition of self-assessment which focuses on the formative learning promoting: Self-assessment is a process of formative assessment during which students reflect on and evaluate the quality of their work and their learning, judge the degree to which they reflect explicitly stated goals or criteria, identify strengths and weaknesses in their work, and revise accordingly.

In general two main purposes of assessment can be given. The first is to provide certification of achievement to graduate with a validation of their performance. Another purpose is to facilitate learning (Andrade, H. & Du, Y., 2007, p.160)

In Figure 6-1 the role of assessment and feedback in a Blended Learning course is pictured. This illustration includes two different aspects. On the one hand, this graphic can be seen from the perspective of learning. In this scenario the learner enlarges his or her knowledge participating in lectures or studying at home using various materials. This learning progress will be evaluated using one or more assessments during the course phase. In the end the students receives the feedback of instructors.

Another perspective could be the teacher's. All the assessments given to the students reflect the quality or only the progress of the course itself. Using additional surveys or questioning the teacher or instructor obtains an assessment of the course given by the students. Both, the results of the assessments as well as of the feedback should help the instructors to improve their teaching.

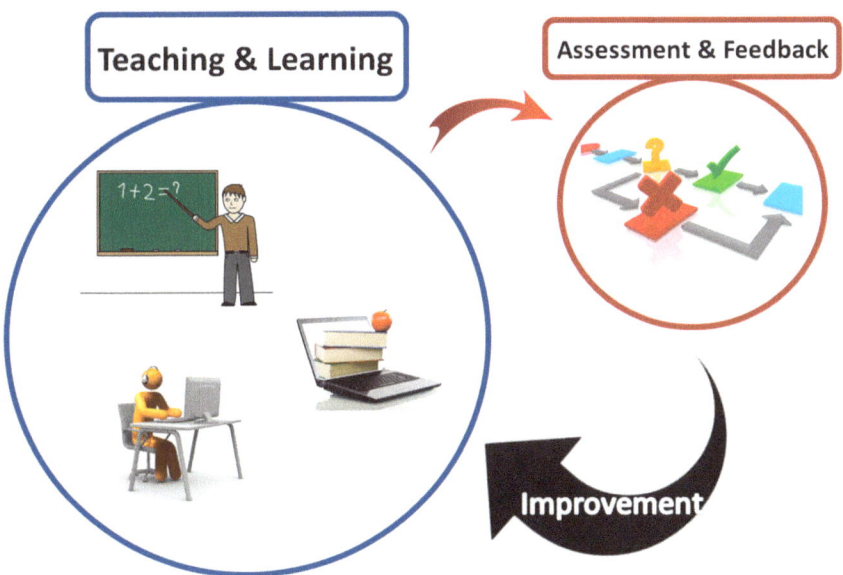

Figure 6-1: Usage of assessment in a Blended Learning course.

6.1. Assessments Classification

6.1.1. Assessment types

Many people might think that assessment is exam in the end of a course to verify the grade of the learner. Assessment is much more variable and multifarious. There are various types of assessments (Ronan, Amanda, 2015 and http://edglossary.org/assessment/)

- **Diagnostic Assessment**:

    These diagnostic tests attempt to estimate or give an idea what the learners already know at the beginning of the course about the addressed topics.

- **Formative Assessment**:

    The formative tests are given throughout the course to quantify the student's progress during the course regarding a certain learning goal.

- **Summative Assessment**:

    This assessment is done in the end of the course or year to determine the knowledge or skills of a certain topic.

- **Norm-referenced Assessment**:

    This kind of assessment compares student's results using a national "norm" or average in order to grade the learners and rank them. Examples for such tests are: SAT, ACT, Iowa Basic Skills Test or other state standardized tests

- **Criterion-referenced Assessment**:

    These tests are constructed to test the students for a standard or specific goal. It is usually used to determine the knowledge about certain chapters or units. An example of this test structure is the SBAC (Smarter Balanced Assessment Consortium).

- **Performance Assessment**:

    For this assessment, learners have to accomplish complex tasks such as speeches, science experiments or long-term projects. Some educators are thinking that this type of assessment is more accurate and meaningful than ordinary evaluations.

- **Placement Assessment**:

    Such tests are used to classify the learners into the correct course level or academic program. If there are language courses for different levels this test would decide, which course a learner has to attend.

- **Screening Assessment**:

    This kind of assessment evaluates if learners are fitting the requirements and provide the needed skills. For example in some universities, there are entrance restrictions, which can be determined using this assessment.

The classification only separates different types of assessments in terms of point in time of the course as well as aim of the test. The choice of the assessment also influences the decision which kind of assignment is the right one to receive an answer to the interesting question if learners reached desired learning goals. It is also possible to rate homework or exercises as a way of an assessment. Generally, speaking everything, which is reviewed or allows a certain statement of the knowledge or skill can be counted as an assessment.

6.1.2. Methods and Question types

In general, different tasks or questions can be used in these different assessments. The following list gives an idea what can be included in a course assessment and which methods and questions can be used:

- **Multiple Choice Questions**:

    This question type offers the learner different possible answers where one or more answers are right. In the test the learner has to decide which answers are correct. This question type can only be used for certain subjects of matter. The instructor has to know the purpose of the question.

- **Fill in the blank Questions**:

    This question type offers an incomplete answer where certain words can be filled in by the learners as an exercise. On the one hand, there can be a collection of some possible as well as wrong answers where the learner has to pick the right one. On the other hand, the learners could be forced to think of the missing words or terms by themselves.

- **Adaptive Questions**:

    This type formulates questions in separated smaller steps. There are two different versions. On the one hand, the smaller steps can help the learners to figure out the solution during the question. On the other hand, it can also be used to create a question where the partial answers build on each other. This second option could be used to evaluate if the learners understand the connection between different subjects.

- **Essays**:

    Depending on the subject of matter, a longer essay or a shorter paragraph can be part of the assignment. This could also include literature work as well as preparing a programming file with a certain function.

- **Presentations**:

    Presentations can be also part of the assessment. For a fair evaluation of the learner's performance, certain guidelines and rating criteria should be defined in advance. Assessing these criteria could be done using rubrics or similar common scoring guides.

The list of methods or questions types might not be complete. The progress in technology and expansion of possibilities offers more experimental assignments which can be included in the course assessment.

6.1.3. Assessment Designs

In the following list some of the different arrangements of assessment are presented. This arrangement can contain all different methods and question types discussed above.

- **Homework**:

    This assessment is periodic, for example weekly. In addition, the timespan for fulfilling the task is usually around a week or more. The focus of the homework is that learners are working by themselves using all the methods they learned in the course and combine it with other sources.

- **Tests & Quizzes**:

    Tests or quizzes can be used for many different purposes. On the one hand, they can be used to perform a diagnostic assessment in the beginning of the course. This can be included in the

development of the course start. On the other hand, tests can also be used to realize formative assessments throughout the course duration. Usually these tests are short and not as complex as exams. These quizzes can also be used to generate a form of self-assessment. This self-assessment itself has two different meanings. The students can have tests, which are graded by the teacher or automatically and draw conclusions of their own knowledge. Or the test can be given to them without any solutions in order to motivate them to evaluate the results on their own. The tests could be done using an online tool as well as using pencil and paper to perform the tasks.

- **Exam**:

An exam is usually used to perform a summative assessment. The learners have to prepare the subject of the whole course and the instructor can assess their knowledge using oral, written or even online exams. The usability of online exams depends on the used environment as well as the subject of the exam.

- **Portfolio**
- The tasks which should be gathered in the portfolio are announced during the semester or altogether at the beginning or in the end. Usually the students have a certain amount of weeks to gather all the materials and design the portfolio. It depends on the didactical aim if a combination with a presentation is useful. This portfolio can be sent in or uploaded as well as handed to the teacher.

- **Seminar Paper**:

Similar to the portfolio the seminar paper needs also a longer preparation time by the learner. It might be combined with a presentation as well. The seminar paper promotes the students to scientific working. Also a solid research in the subject area is required.

6.1.4. Feedback

In order to guarantee a successful and well evaluated course not only the assessment of the learners but also the assessment of the course itself is important. As described in Figure 1 this course evaluation can be done by the learners in different forms of feedback.

- **Discussion**:

This feedback enables learners to discuss problems with structure or tasks in the course as a group. The instructor gets an overview of the opinion of the students. This discussion can be prepared but might lead to completely different topics, which are important for the learner but have not been considered by the instructor.

- **Questionnaire**:

An anonymous questionnaire or survey helps the instructor to find answers to very specific questions, which should fit to the learning goals. It helps to evaluate the feeling of the students independent of the marks of the assessments during the course. If the group of learners is big enough also statistical evaluations are possible.

- **Interview**:

The questionnaire might be done publicly. Therefore, the instructor knows who made which answers or suggestions. Regarding the evaluation of the course, a combination of a questionnaire with an interview afterwards might be the best solution. Using this format the instructor can go into detail if the answer in the questionnaire is not enough.

6.2. Assessment at TU Wien

At the TU Wien different assessments are realized. As mentioned in Chapter 5.2 there are different mathematical courses offered. All the courses have different requirements and therefore the course structure is adjusted to the conditions and learning goals of these courses.

6.2.1. Refresher Course

The refresher course is held at the beginning of the first semester. Seven different fields of studies can attend this course. Due to the fact that this course is offered to 2000 students and the timetable is very tight the administration and practicing has to be done efficiently. The course is held in two rotations. One is starting in the second half of September. Students who are able to attend this cycle are not parallel dealing with the semester start in October. For all students who are just arriving in Vienna with the start of the semester a second cycle is offered. A disadvantage is the overwhelming administrational effort of all simultaneously starting lectures.

Both courses take 7-14 days. Therefore the structure has to be very simple. The topics are separated in different modules. This enables students to participate in selected modules where they need to refresh their school knowledge. After two hour lecture the students can go to the following exercise. Compared to the lecture where 200 to 400 students are sitting the exercises are held in smaller groups of up to 60 people. Every group has its own tutor who explains and practices the methods heard in the lecture.

Additionally to the lecture and exercise the course is administrated using a Moodle platform. There the students find all important information from the time table and the module description through all the lecture and exercise materials. There are various online examples where the students can practice and get a feeling for their knowledge level. At the end of every module the students have the possibility to make a quiz in order to assess their skills.

In order to complete the course successfully the students have to pass a final exam. This final exam is performed on an online environment. This requires a certain amount of tutors guarding the examination process. It would not be possible to perform this exam at home. Additionally there is a prep-exam to help the students during the learning process for the final exam.

Regarding feedback there is also a diagnostic test which is done in the first exercise. This test shows students which modules they should attend before the semester starts. The results of this test can be compared and statistically evaluated using the final exam. Additionally an anonymous survey is realized to gather information regarding educational background and mathematical self-evaluation after the course.

6.2.2. Basic and Advanced Mathematical Courses

In the basic and advanced mathematical courses the situation is more relaxed. The lectures are four times a week throughout the semester. The lecture is a teacher-centered lecture and closes with a final exam. There are no additional assessments during the semester.

In the parallel exercises, which are, once a week the methods and knowledge from the lecture is tested. Every week the students have to prepare at least 6 of 10 examples in order to present them in front of a tutor. Additionally there are online examples provided to deepen the understanding.

In the middle of the course a survey is done anonymously to gather learning results as well as structural or executing problems. The evaluation of the survey can be used to improve the currently running course.

Distributed over the semester there are three tests executed on the online system. The students have to pass two of three tests. These tests should show them which part of the exercise they understood. These tests are also preparation for the final lecture exam. In addition, this exam is done in the online system.

The variety of assessments in these courses should support the students during their learning process individually.

6.2.3. Simulation Courses

The simulation courses are a combination of lecture and projects. The students have two lectures a week. One of these lectures explains modelling and simulation principles the other one gives the student an understanding of applying different methods for various simulation applications.

This lecture is supported by an e-learning environment where the students can experiment with different simulation application. It is also possible to look at the underlying algorithms in order to improve their programming skills.

The lecture ends one month before the semester to give students time to start with their projects. This project is an application of the learned methods. The students gather in small groups of 2-3 to develop the model. In the end, the students perform a presentation of their work and summarize the work in a protocol. Using this assessment structure different skills are required and should be combined to perform the task properly.

6.3. Summary

Formative assessments are commonly said to be *for* learning because educators use the results to modify and improve teaching techniques during an instructional period, while summative assessments are said to be *of* learning because they evaluate academic achievement at the conclusion of an instructional period. Or - as assessment expert Paul Black put it - "When the cook tastes the soup, that's formative assessment. When the customer tastes the soup, that's summative assessment."

6.3.1. Quality of Assessment

In order to ensure a high quality of the course several quality criteria worked out in the previous chapter should be considered.

As mentioned in section 4.3 it is important to communicate which knowledge is required for the course. Regarding assessment also the ICT skills are important to announce at the beginning. If there are problems using the assessment environment a certain tutorial support should be provided. In section 5.5 the requirements regarding tutorial support are listed.

Regarding all the quality criteria one of the most important aspects is to explain the procedure and the assessment structure to the students. They have to know how the course will be graded in the beginning of the course in order to design a personal learning plan. What will be part of the assessment, when and how will it be performed. For example, the refresher course structure was modified over the past years to offer various learning paths. The information about the exams is explained in the first lecture. All the practice tools are shown in the lecture and there are also hands-on exercises to get to know the system.

Another important part mentioned in Chapter 5 concerns the feedback for students. It does not matter which assessment is chosen if it fits the purpose. But it is very important to provide a proper feedback. On the one hand, it could be an automatic feedback. The advantage is the response time. The second students finish the assessment they get the results. The disadvantage might be that the automatic feedback does not show many

details and it is not possible to ask back. Therefore, automatic feedbacks should be combined with consultation-hours. If there is no automatic evaluation the time span between assessment and feedback is critical. It should be as short as possible: The feedback should be detailed to suggest the students what the results of the assessment means to their learning progress.

It is also important to include the learners in the grading process if it is not an automatic grading. According to Hounsell (2003) the development of assessment should go in direction of "student involvement in the generation of feedback, and a more open and collaborative approach to assignments".

Without any doubt these are not all quality criteria but they are the most important ones to guarantee the maximum output of the course for the learners.

6.3.2. Choice of Assessment

Before choosing the adequate form of assessment the instructor has to clarify the purpose and goal of the assessment. This question should be answered before designing a test or a task. If the educator is not aware what the result of the assessment should evaluate the assessment is useless.

If the purpose of the assessment is evaluated the right form of assessment can be designed. This planning phase should be included in the course design due to the fact that different assessments require a certain time span the time table of the course structure could be influenced.

Table 1 combines all the different parameters which are important to consider in the assessment design. It can also be seen as a checklist. For example the administration part might be depending on the facility where the assessment is done. The facility also influences the possible location of the assessment. The execution as well as the time span and point in time of the assignment are related to the choice of the assessment type as written in 6.1.1.

Location	Execution	Timespan	Point in Time	Grading	Administration
Lecture Hall	oral	20 minutes	daily	self-evalution	In Person
Seminar Room	written	2 hours	once a week	peer assessment	Via Email
EDV-Labor	online	one week	once a month	automatically	Homepage
at Home	combination	one semester	once in course	by teacher	Learning Platform

Table 6-1: Checklist for designing an assessment

The decision about the grading depends on the didactical goal of the assessment. The subject and appropriate question types as well as methods are critical for the grading.

All these different adaptations influence the purpose and result of the assessment. All the factors should be considered carefully to provide a perfectly designed Blended Learning course.

Sources

Andrade, H. & DU, Y. (2007). "Student responses to criteria-referenced self-assessment". Assessment and Evaluation of Higher Education, 32(2), p. 159-181

Boud, D. & Falchikov, N. (2006). "Aligning assessment with long-term learning". Assessment and Evaluation of Higher Education, 31(4), p. 399-413

Boud, D. (1995). "Enhancing learning trough self-assessment". London: Kogan Page.

Govindasamy, T. (2002). "Sucessful implementation of e-Learning Pedagogical considerations". Internet and Higher Education, 4, p. 287-299

Hounsell, D. (2003) "Student feedback, learning and development". M. Slowey & D. Watson (Eds) Higher education and the lifecourse (Buckingham, Society for Research into Higher Education & Open University Press), p. 67–78.

Ismail, J. (2002). "The design of an e-learning system beyond the hype". Internet and Higher Education, 4, p. 329-336

Ronan, Amanda (2015).Edudemic.connecting education & technology", http://www.edudemic.com/summative-and-formative-assessments/

Chapter 7:
The Pilot Course

Authored by: Annika Meder-Liikanen (University of Helsinki)
Merja Auvinen (University of Helsinki)
Ari Myllyviita (University of Helsinki)

Contents of Chapter 7

7. The Pilot Course	105
7.1. Structure of the test course	108
7.1.1. First face-to-face session (January 26, 2015)	108
7.1.2. Online period (January – May)	110
7.1.3. Second face-to-face session, May 15-16, 2015	111
7.2. The outcomes of the test course	112
7.3. Reinforcing and completing the quality criteria	112
7.4. Attachments:	114

List of Figures

Figure 7-1: The Blended Learning course structure	108
Figure 7-2: Slide from the presentations	112
Figure 7-3: Results of reinforcing and completing the institutional quality criteria	114
Figure 7-4: Results of reinforcing and completing the enrolment quality criteria	114
Figure 7-5: Results of reinforcing and completing the course quality criteria	115
Figure 7-6: Results of reinforcing and completing the learning environment quality criteria	116
Figure 7-7: Results of reinforcing and completing the assessment and evaluation quality criteria	117

List of Tables

Table 7-1: Participants, their teaching subjects and home towns	105
Table 7-2: Learning platform –comparison	106
Table 7-3: The pre-course questionnaire	107
Table 7-4: The pre-course questionnaire	108
Table 7-5: Programme of the first f2f meeting	110
Table 7-6: Programme of the second face-to-face meeting	112

7. The Pilot Course

As part of the project "Quality in Blended Learning" (WP 6) a group of teachers and teacher educators from Helsinki University Viikki Teacher Training School designed and carried out a test course on blended learning quality from January to May 2015. The test course was realized as a further education in-service course for experienced subject and class teachers from different parts of Finland. The participants earned five credits from the course.

Olli Aho	Head Teacher of a Primary School	Porvoo
Niklas Läckström	Class teacher	Porvoo
Eija Huostila-Hällström	Class teacher	Porvoo
Maarit Kostamo	French and English teacher	Kouvola
Terhi Hinkkanen	Home economics teacher	Helsinki
Manna Parvinen	English teacher	Helsinki
Anna-Kaisa Marjamaa	Class Teacher	Oulu
Taina Arkimo	French teacher	Helsinki
Ann-Marie Tavaila	PE and Health Education teacher	Helsinki
Anu Hyrkkänen	PE and health education teacher	Helsinki

Table 7-1: Participants, their teaching subjects and home towns

Developing the test course structure was carried out in a working team of eight QBL project members, co-ordinators, project participants and teacher educators. Several pedagogical points of view were discussed during this process. The background information and surveys from the other "Quality in Blended Learning" work packages were taken carefully into consideration when planning the course. The planning was based on the quality criteria items developed as a result from the research work:

1. Institutional quality
2. Enrolment
3. Course quality
4. Learning environment and learning phase
5. Assessment and evaluation.

This also affected the structure of the course. For example, learning profoundly about blended learning quality would require using learner-centered blended learning methods in the teaching and learning process.

Our pedagogical approach was based on the fact that knowledge about blended learning quality should be built in close collaboration with the tutors, participants and project members. The existing materials (work packages) formed the basis on which knowledge construction was founded. The participants of the test course were active operators themselves in their own learning process; they planned, designed and carried out their own teaching experiments in their own schools and with their own students and pupils after familiarizing themselves with the quality criteria. Afterwards the quality criteria were reinforced and re-evaluated based on their own experiences as teachers, tutors and students of the pilot course.

Before starting the pilot course, we considered several possible online learning platforms. Finally, we chose an online tutoring platform called Edmodo due to its versatility and flexibility. Edmodo is very easy to use for

both the tutor and the learner. In addition, it is free for educational purposes. The teacher trainers and course designers had used it earlier with their own groups of students and pupils, so we knew the good sides and the limitations of the platform already. The participants, new tutors-to-be themselves, were taught the basics of Edmodo prior to the course of course. Edmodo is free, easy to manage by teacher, quite simple to use, so the basics could be adopted in a short tutoring session and some individual practice. We started advertising the course in different online forums about a month before the beginning of the course. After enrollment, the participants were given a preliminary pre-course questionnaire to fill in. The questionnaire focused on the participants' expectations for the course, prior experience in blended learning and their tutoring preferences. Based on the information collected, the test course structure and contents were further modified to meet the participants´ needs.

Table 7-2: Learning platform –comparison

Question Prompt: 7
Total Points: 1

Mitä verkkotyökaluja käytät tällä hetkellä?

Question Prompt: 8
Total Points: 15
Points per answer: 1

Olen käyttänyt seuraavia toimintaympäristöjä (merkitse rastilla x jos olet käyttänyt ja pikku o-kirjaimella, jos et ole käyttänyt): Edmodo _____, Wiki _____, Blogi _____, GAFE (Google application for education) _____, Peda.net _____, Edu20 (NEOLMS) _____ , Office 365 _____, Fronter _____, Moodle _____, Optima _____, Yammer _____, Facebook _____, Second Life _____, BlackBoard _____, Tai joku muu (mikä) _____.

Question Prompt: 9
Total Points: 1

Mihin tutor-ryhmään haluat? Huomioi, että eräät palvelut tarvitsevat tiettyjä sähköpostiosoitteita ja esim. GAFE edellyttää omassa käytössä koulun domainin käyttöä (jos domainia käytetään jo muussa yhteydessä, täytyy mahdollisesti valita toinen). Näihin kyllä palataan lähitapaamisessa.

- ☐ Edmodo kielten opetuksessa
- ☐ Edmodo ja jatkuva arviointi
- ☐ Peda.net: muokattavat oppikirjat, oppimisympäristön räätälöinti
- ☐ Wikit: yhteisöllinen reaaliaikainen tiedon tuottaminen ja jakaminen
- ☐ Blogit: Oppimisprosessin kuvaus ja vertaisarviointi
- ☐ GAFE - Google application for Education

Question Prompt: 10

Table 7-3: The pre-course questionnaire

7.1. Structure of the test course

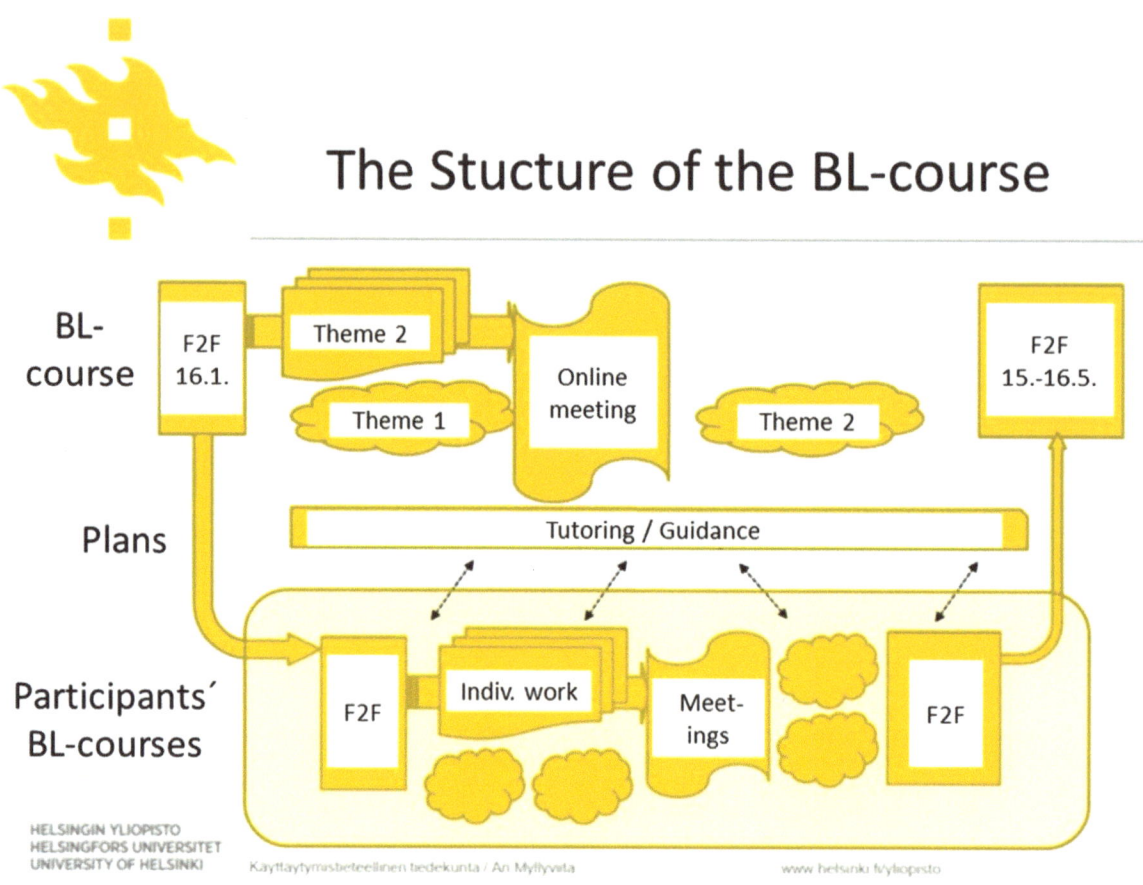

Figure 7-1: The Blended Learning course structure

The test course consisted of two face-to-face sessions and an online period. The face-to-face sessions were run at the beginning (January) and at the end of the course (May), the online period taking place in between. During the online period, the participants carried out their own teaching experiments using the blended learning methods most suitable for their own purposes.

For the teaching experiments, the participants were allowed to choose from a variety of online platforms the one that would best meet their needs. The options offered were Edmodo, Wikis, GAFE (Google Apps for Education), PedaNet and blogs for educational purposes. We offered tutoring for both the technical and pedagogical use of these platforms. This was carried out both in the face- to-face sessions and on the Edmodo platform during the online period.

Wikis	3 participants (class teachers)
GAFE	5 participants (1 class teacher, 3 subject teachers)
Edmodo	4 participants (3 language teachers)

Table 7-4: The pre-course questionnaire

7.1.1. First face-to-face session (January 26, 2015)

The first face-to-face meeting took place in January, 2015.

The day started with the introductions of the QBL Project members, tutors, participants and the QiBL project management. The Project Manager Luca Reitano introduced himself and the whole project via Skype.

The quality criteria from the QBL work packages were introduced, defined and discussed.

We were also lucky to have a Dutch expert on blended learning, Dr Nanda van der Stap from the University of Utrecht, with us to give us a webinar on "Experiences on Blended Learning Quality".

The tutors then presented the various online platforms and tools to be used in the course and the quality criteria for the learning platform. The participants were able to choose the platform and tools that they found most suitable for their own teaching experiments. The small groups were then formed accordingly.

The learning platform to be used during the course with the whole group, Edmodo, was introduced.

In the afternoon we works in small groups planning the online period work in detail with the tutor of the group, taking the participants' own goals and needs into consideration, deepening the technical and pedagogical knowledge of the online learning platform to be used in their teaching experiment. The initial plans were documented on Edmodo. WP 5 material and the quality criteria were discussed in detail.

Friday, January 16, 2015

8.45 am	Welcome and coffee (Room LUO, 3rd floor)
9.00 am	Introductions. Quality in Blended Learning Project and the Work Packages http://bit.ly/106JEcY /Ari Myllyviita
9.30 am	The quality criteria in blended learning (Room STU, 3rd floor)
	WP 1 Research + materials : http://bit.ly/1tun879J / Ari Myllyviita
	WP 2 Quality Criteria + materials: http://bit.ly/ZZ1nTA / Merja Auvinen, Ari Myllyviita
9.50 am	**A Webinar** on the Experiences on Blended Learning Courses (University of Applied Science, Utrecht)
10.30 am	Using different online tools in the classroom, case studies/ the trainers/tutoring teachers
	WP 4 Quality criteria for the learning platform / Annika Meder-Liikanen
12.00	Lunch (School Cafeteria, 1st floor)
12.45 pm	**The Steering Group of the QiBL** introductions/Luca Reitano /Skype video meeting
1.15 pm	How to use the Edmodo platform? A brief introduction / Merja Auvinen, Annu Ojala, Annmarie Tavaila
2.00 pm	Coffee break
-4.00 pm	**Working in the tutor groups:** Wikis - Collaborative Knowledge Production and Sharing / Peter von Bonsdorff, Ari Myllyviita (Room LUO)
	1. Pedanet – Personal Learning Management Systems / Tapani Saarinen, Ari myllyviita (Room 2061)
	2. Edmodo in Foreign Language Learning / Merja Auvinen, Annu Ojala (Room EN1)

> 3. Blogs – the Learning Process and Peer Evaluation / Reetta Nisonen, Annika Meder-Liikanen (Room STU)
> 4. Edmodo and Process Assessment and Feedback /Anu Hyrkkänen, Annmarie Tavaila, Ari Myllyviita (Room KA1)
> 5. GAFE – Google Application for Education /Mika Parviainen (Room Ki1)
>
> **WP 5 Quality Criteria for tutoring + materials**
>
> **Agreeing on the practical issues of the online period**, based on the quality criteria defined, e.g.
>
> - Expectations of the participants, the participants' prior knowledge
> - Communication, the number of contacts during the online working period
> - The cycles of the online period (weeks, dates)
> - Cooperation (group work, feedback from peers as well)
> - The duties of the participants and the trainers
> - The expected outcome
> - The background material to be used during the online period / Flipped Classroom: copyright issues, the role of ICT in the curricula, etc.
> - The initial plans for the participants' own BL courses

Table 7-5: Programme of the first f2f meeting

7.1.2. Online period (January – May)

After the first face-to-face meeting, we had three expert tutors working with a small group of three to four course participants. Each group used a different platform or online tools:

1. The Wiki / Office 365 group with one tutor and three participants
2. The GAFE group with one tutor and five participants
3. The Edmodo for language teachers group with two tutors and four participants.

All the small groups planned their work together in detail. Each group also agreed how the online tutoring would be best carried out to suit the timetables of the participants' courses, what kind of support the participants would be needing to carry out their own teaching experiments with blended learning.

We organized one online meeting during the online working period focusing on blended learning copyright issues. The participants were asked to watch an online video lecture on copyright issues given by one of the leading experts on the topic in Finland, then answer some tricky questions in their own Edmodo small group discussion forum. After that, there was an online video meeting where the participants were able to ask the lecturer more questions and discuss the issue more.

The second online meeting was an asynchronous one: the participants watched a PP presentation on the role of ICT in the new, ongoing curriculum reform in Finland. Each small group then discussed the topic in their small groups in Edmodo.

The most important thing for all the participants was naturally to design their own teaching experiment with their own students or pupils in detail, carry them out in their own institutes and prepare to present them in the face-to-face meeting in May. Throughout this time they had regular online support from their tutors and from their group.

7.1.3. Second face-to-face session, May 15-16, 2015

The second face-to-face meeting was organized in mid-May after a meeting day with the QBL steering group members (Peter Mazohl, Harald Makl, Nikolaos Tzimopoulos and Vangelis Hiliadis), the Finnish project coordinators and test course tutors. On the actual meeting day, all the project participants were also present of course.

We discussed the quality criteria again in detail, both in the initial lectures and when the participants introduced their teaching experiments using blended learning tools. What in particular improved the quality of the courses? Was there anything that worked in the opposite way?

A lot of time was spent on assessment and self-evaluation, re-evaluating and completing the quality criteria using some more online tools, e.g. Presemo and Kahoot (see below in 7.3). Potential follow-up work and future cooperation was discussed as well.

All the participants were interviewed by the steering group members.

Here the program of the meeting:

Fri 15 May 2014 9.30 am to 4 pm in "STUDIO"	
Presenting the teaching experiments and evaluation	
9.30	Morning assembly in the auditorium
9.45	Morning coffee in STUDIO
10.00	QiBl group members introduction: experiences on blended learning, Quality criteria recap (Nikos XX and Vangelis XX, Greece, Peter Mazohl and Harald Makl, Austria)
10.45	Test course participants present their teaching experiments carried out during the spring. WIKIS Office 365 & GAFE & EDMODO LANGUAGES o The structure of the teaching experiment; what, how, who, when etc. o Quality point of view; what increased and decreased teaching and learning quality during the teaching experiment?
12.00	LUNCH & COFFEE
12.45	Presentations by course participants continue WIKIS Office 365 & GAFE & EDMODO LANGUAGES
2 pm	Assessment, self evaluation, discussing and completing the quality criteria. (Test course participants, tutors and QiBl group members together. Presemo/Annika) Short interviews with participants (Harald Makl & Vangelis X)
2.45	Questionnaire (Peter Mazohl & Nikos X)
2.50	Course Feedback. (Tool: Kahoot/Reetta)
3.15	QiBL group member comments on the course (Peter, Mazohl Nikolaos Tzimopoulos, Harald Makl, Vangelis Hiliadis) Focus round.
3.45	Handing out course diplomas, official photo

4 pm	Meeting ends

Table 7-6: Programme of the second face-to-face meeting

7.2. The outcomes of the test course

The course offered both the tutors and the participants' valuable insights into blended learning quality. We feel this kind of hands-on approach where theory is immediately put into practice through individual teaching experiments serves as an excellent springboard for an open discussion on the quality criteria of blended learning. We very much recommend this kind of double approach for all introductory courses on blended learning.

During the second face-to-face session, the participants presented their own teaching experiments. There were twelve participants from different parts of Finland; Kouvola, Porvoo, Oulu and Helsinki. All teaching experiments had different target groups, goals and different outcomes. There was also variation in the age of the students. This was very interesting and gave versatile insights to blended learning quality issues. The experiments were all presented on the final training day and described also on the Edmodo working area for everyone to concentrate on after the course as well.

7.3. Reinforcing and completing the quality criteria

The quality in Blended Learning

- **Leadership** – how to manage the group
- How manage with **people** – choose wisely the communication tool – should it be the one you want to learn to use
- **Policy** – do what you need to do, not something else
- Check all **resources** you need – what students need
- The **process** is based on the context of the real world
    - You have to try what you are studying (BL)
    - Don´t try just "something", make the real thing
    - Make your own timetable
- THEN WE HAVE RESULTS

Merja Auvinen & Ari Myllyviita / Aug 28, 2015
Malaga Conference

Figure 7-2: Slide from the presentations

The quality is based on understanding of the process and the context. Well designed management and leadership, well planned, how people are linked together (a valid communication tool), aware of needed resources, context based process – learning by doing.

During the test course, the quality criteria from WP 2 (Institution quality, enrollment quality, Course quality, Learning Environment quality and Assessment and evaluation quality) were discussed, re-evaluated and completed. This was done to discuss the quality criteria from the participants´ point of view on the basis of their own teaching experiments. This was an important part of the pedagogical point of view of the whole test course; the approach was very learner-oriented from the very beginning, the participants were included

in the knowledge construction process throughout the course, and they were active operators in their own learning process. They learned how to plan, design, choose the most appropriate tools to serve their own purposes, carry out and evaluate their own blended learning experiment course.

Reinforcing and completing the quality criteria was done in the second face-to-face meeting using an audience activating online tool called Presemo[34]. Similar activating features can be found, for example, on many other online tools, eg. Socrative[35].

With this tool, the participants were able to add their own suggestions to the list of the criteria and vote for the most important quality issues. The results of this work can be seen in the images below. The criteria and the work was divided into five categories; institution, enrollment, course quality, learning environment and assessment/evaluation.

---

[34] http://presemo.com/

[35] http://socrative.com/

7.4. Attachments

Read through the Institutional quality factors. Discuss them with the person sitting next to you and add points of view that are missing in your opinion. What should be taken into consideration in addition from the institution's point of view?

-

Pisteet:

(3) e-course content completeness
(3) Curriculum in active use - blended learning always in connected to the curriculum
(3) Pedagogy
(2) Instructional Design
(2) Resources of the institution / Course provider; Technical, Human and Financial
(2) Useable platform
(2) Naming institutional goals
(2) Helpdesk
(2) Copyright issues are taken into consideration
(2) Own real project / task
(2) The institution's policy is to offer a learner-centered access to teaching
(2) Open what criterias mean in terms of quality
(1) Administration: Technical Administration, Program Administration
(1) Teachers/Trainers ICT Skills and Didactic Skills
(1) Working infrastucture, wlan
(1) Allocating tasks (who's doing what)
(1) agreed curriculum (content, mission, ...)
(1) Leading group - division of resbonsilities
(0) Documentation (Documentation Control, Course, Materials, Reports ...)
(0) Clear
(0) The institution has wide networks and is active in networking
(0) A system for collecting feedback from students

Figure 7-3: Results of reinforcing and completing the institutional quality criteria

What are important quality factors when carrying out enrollment for a blended learning course? Read through the existing criteria (marked with a #). Discuss with the person sitting next to you: what could be added? Is there a point of view missing that should be taken into consideration? Send one factor at a time.

-

Pisteet:

(6) Information about the course contents and goals
(4) Timetable
(4) assessment criteria
(4) added value for learning
(3) #easy access to software and materials
(2) #pre-information about the structure of the course
(2) getting the students to set their own goals for the course
(2) expectations of members
(1) #participants' pre-knowledge
(1) #knowledge of participants' ict skills
(1) equipment needed
(1) evaluation
(0) #registration system
(0) #enrollment handling
(0) Informing students' parents (esp. with younger students)
(0) deadline
(0) copyright issues
(0) recuired preknowledge
(0) netiquette
(0) individual protection issues
(0) development during course
(0) group division
(0) rules for when the teacher can be contacted
(0) documentation (eg materials, feedback system)

Figure 7-4: Results of reinforcing and completing the enrolment quality criteria

A guidance to Blended Learning

> What are important quality factors in a blended learning course itself? Read through the existing criteria (marked with a #). Discuss with the person sitting next to you: what could be added? Is there a point of view missing that should be taken into consideration? Send one criteria at a time.
>
> Pisteet:
>
> (7) interaction
> (4) back up contact and motivational support
> (3) authentic material, currect issues
> (3) Platform that works on different devices
> (3) setting your own goals
> (2) #documentation of the course
> (2) Continuous evaluation
> (2) ICT support
> (2) peer learning
> (2) diversification
> (1) #Well known course structure and (necessary) resources
> (1) peer contact and discussions
> (1) Giving the student the possibility to advance according to their own skill level
> (1) Added value for learning
> (1) giving the students the possibility to have a say about the course contents
> (1) active tutoring online
> (1) Platform that's easy to use
> (1) using varied assessment methods
> (0) #course development
> (0) #instructional design
> (0) #Get to know the tutor(s)/teacher(s) and the other learners
> (0) #Use of technology
> (0) help available - when and how
> (0) one plus one is more
> (0) current issues
> (0) Self evaluation and feedback from teacher
> (0) plan for drop out prevention

Figure 7-5: Results of reinforcing and completing the course quality criteria

What are important quality factors in a learning environment on a blended learning course? Read through the existing criteria (marked with a #). Discuss with the person sitting next to you: what could be added? Is there a point of view missing that should be taken into consideration? Send one criteria at a time.

Pisteet:

(8) Platform that is easy to use
(6) Visually and emotionally inviting platform
(5) portfolios for individual students taking different courses
(3) #Getting students engaged
(3) Platform that works on different devices
(3) versatile
(3) multi task and useage possible
(3) Clearly structured files for different types of tasks
(2) #Motivation: External controlled motivation and Self determined motivation
(2) #Communication
(2) easy to use
(1) #Maintain enduring engage ment
(1) #Learning platform
(1) #Equipment & Software
(1) #Platform for the distance learning phase
(0) #Re - engaging students who drift away or fail to engage
(0) #Technical Learning Environment
(0) #Additional issues
(0) #Student support
(0) #Tutorial support
(0) #Workload
(0) #Technology
(0) a visually appealing platform
(0) new tools possible to implement
(0) Giving the teacher a quiz tool that corrects itself

Figure 7-6: Results of reinforcing and completing the learning environment quality criteria

A guidance to Blended Learning

> What are important quality factors when carrying out assessment and evaluation on a blended learning course? Read through the existing criteria (marked with a #). Discuss with the person sitting next to you: what could be added? Is there a point of view missing that should be taken into consideration? Send one criteria at a time.
>
> -
>
> Pisteet:
>
> (5) Evaluation must be based on the set goals
> (5) Peer evaluation should be easy
> (5) the possibility to assess progress and the fact of learning new things during the course
> (5) continuous assessment
> (4) peer assessment in addition to teacher's assessment
> (3) using different types of testing
> (3) different ways to assess for different learners
> (3) Teacher's feedback should always be in the same place and easily accesible
> (2) criteria understandable
> (1) #Evaluation criteria (course provider's view as well as learner's view)
> (1) the possibility to receive and discuss feedback of assessment
> (0) #Planning and Definition
> (0) #Assessment execution
> (0) #Validation of the course (learner's view)
> (0) assessment troughout the course

Figure 7-7: Results of reinforcing and completing the assessment and evaluation quality criteria

8. Conclusions

Experience showed that fostering quality teaching is a multi-level endeavor.

Fabrice Hénard and Deborah Roseveare

Quality matters – especially in teaching. High quality teaching may lead to better learning results. When we use special teaching techniques like Blended Learning this is naturally an important issue. Talking about quality, we should address a range of questions:

- What do we mean with quality assurance and which approach can we chose?
- What are the stakeholders or players in quality assurance?
- Which quality assurance systems are currently used or valid for us in Europe?
- How can quality assurance be implemented in a teaching institution?
- What is the benefit of quality assurance for the learners?

These and some more questions could be asked when you plan high quality Blended Learning. The consortium could find some answers to the questions mentioned above. Because of workshops, discussions, conferences, surveys and the studies of "lessons learned" from numerous various eLearning and Blended Learning courses performed by the consortium members an appropriate quality framework was developed with a special focus on the learners' needs. The starting point of all considerations was the Adult Learner, but the consortium found out that – except of the problem of the maturity of the learner – almost all facts and descriptions of the quality framework are relevant for VET or Higher Education as well.

8.1. Why use a quality framework?

Quality frameworks are well defined quality assurance systems with an open description and must adapted to the individual case of the teaching situation (that may depend on the teaching institution, the subject or a special teaching condition in a special course group). In some way quality frameworks can be seen as a description of an open system, covering the summary of all quality assurance items and the user (educator, teaching organisation or educational unit) has to select the necessary and relevant items for their teaching activity.

8.2. How to use the developed quality framework?

The developed framework offers a versatile description of quality fields, which complete the existing ISO/IEC standards with the necessary items, which are in context with the learners' needs. These needs were taken as the starting point of the considerations for quality criteria and brought to a list of quality criteria fitting to the quality fields.

The various quality criteria offer a set of versatile access methods for quality assurance. The quality criteria cover the complete teaching process in a Blended Learning environment. Here the process of Blended Learning is in the foreground, other issues like pedagogical aspects or the cooperation of learners or peer groups ate not topic of the project.

8.3. Future steps

Blended Learning needs a pedagogy (Leo Casey 2011). From that – without doubt correct - point of view further research must be undertaken to find a well-fitting pedagogy for Blended Learning. Besides that the quality framework must be enhanced and cover the pedagogical issues as well. A second step is the practical implementation of such a learning environment.

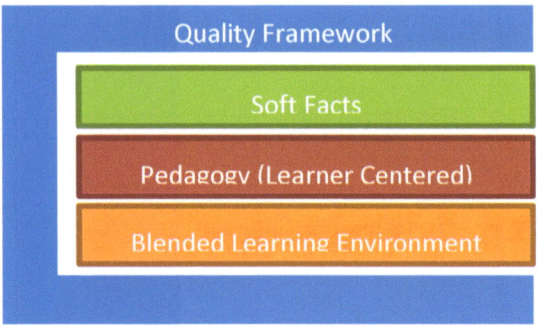

Figure 8-1: *Quality Framework for a complete Blended Learning Environment*

In the graphics above so-called soft facts are also mentioned, these are items like the taught subject or the structure of the peer group (of learners).

The consortium is going to continue the undertaken activities in the frame of the project and to do further research and practical work to develop Blended Learning in a very satisfying way.

Sources

Casey, Leo; Kyofuna, Sara (Eds.) (2011): Finding Pedagogy for Blended Learning. International Conference on Engaging Pedagogy. Dublin, 16/12/2011. Dublin, checked on 9/23/2015.

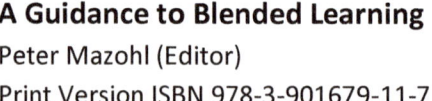

A Guidance to Blended Learning
Peter Mazohl (Editor)
Print Version ISBN 978-3-901679-11-7